Document-Based
Assessment Activities
for U. S. History Classes

Kenneth Hilton

J. WESTON
WALCH
PUBLISHER

Portland, Maine

Acknowledgments

The author wishes to thank all of the publishers who granted permission to use the quotations and illustrations that help bring history to life in this book.

User's Guide
to
Walch Reproducible Books

As part of our general effort to provide educational materials that are as practical and economical as possible, we have designated this publication a "reproducible book." The designation means that purchase of the book includes purchase of the right to limited reproduction of all pages on which this symbol appears:

Here is the basic Walch policy: We grant to individual purchasers of this book the right to make sufficient copies of reproducible pages for use by all students of a single teacher. This permission is limited to a single teacher and does not apply to entire schools or school systems, so institutions purchasing the book should pass the permission on to a single teacher. Copying of the book or its parts for resale is prohibited.

Any questions regarding this policy or requests to purchase further reproduction rights should be addressed to:

Permissions Editor
J. Weston Walch, Publisher
321 Valley Street • P. O. Box 658
Portland, Maine 04104-0658

Contents

Introduction .... *v*
    What Is a Document-based Question? .... *v*
    How to Use and Teach DBQ's .... *vi*
    Getting Started: Guidelines for Students .... *vii*
    How Are Answers Scored? A Scoring Rubric .... *viii*

Unit 1: THE COLONIAL PERIOD
    DBQ 1: Immigration 1
    DBQ 2: Economic Opportunities 6

Unit 2: REVOLUTION, CONFEDERATION, CONSTITUTION
    DBQ 3: Causes of the Revolutionary War 11
    DBQ 4: Ratifying the Constitution 17

Unit 3: THE NEW NATION
    DBQ 5: Growth of Political Parties 23
    DBQ 6: The War of 1812 27

Unit 4: JACKSON, REFORM, AND EXPANSION
    DBQ 7: Jacksonian Democracy 33
    DBQ 8: Antebellum Reforms 39

Unit 5: CIVIL WAR AND RECONSTRUCTION
    DBQ 9: What Caused Secession? 44
    DBQ 10: Reconstruction's Failure 50

Unit 6: A NATION IN TRANSITION
    DBQ 11: The Industrial Boom 57
    DBQ 12: The Nativist Response to Immigration 63

Unit 7: POPULISTS AND PROGRESSIVES
    DBQ 13: The Farmers' Revolt 69
    DBQ 14: Progressivism 74

Unit 8: WORLD EXPANSION AND NEW RESPONSIBILITIES
    DBQ 15: The Debate Over American Imperialism 80
    DBQ 16: Why Did We Enter World War I? 85

Unit 9: PROSPERITY AND DEPRESSION: BETWEEN THE WARS
    DBQ 17: A National Clash of Cultures in the 1920's 90
    DBQ 18: The New Deal's Opponents 95

Unit 10: AMERICA'S LAST 50 YEARS
    DBQ 19: How Has America Changed Since 1950? 102
    DBQ 20: The Civil Rights Movement—
    America's Second Reconstruction 109

Unit 11: TODAY AND TOMORROW—YOUR PLACE IN HISTORY
    DBQ 21: "What Then Is the American?" 117
    DBQ 22: What Does the Future Hold for You? 122

Introduction

Historians, just like detectives, often must reach conclusions with only fragments of evidence and very few clues. They examine what evidence they have, question its relevance to the case, and try to assess its validity. Then, after weighing this evidence against what they already know about the topic, they formulate tentative answers, which they scrutinize and test even further. Being a "detective" about the past is challenging, engaging, and fascinating work. And it's important to remind ourselves that what we often accept as historical "truth" is always being reexamined and questioned, with new interpretations and new theories constantly emerging.

History is not an exact science with "right" and "wrong" answers to every question. Indeed, it can be argued that there are exact answers to only the unimportant and trivial historical questions. Yes, Robert E. Lee's horse was named Traveler. Most of the truly significant questions in history, however, defy pat answers. What factors motivated European settlement of America in the seventeenth century? How important was the antislavery movement in bringing on the Civil War? How could Louis XVI or Czar Nicholas II have been so blind to the need for social and political reforms in their countries? How successful was President Franklin D. Roosevelt's New Deal program in ending the Great Depression? What role, if any, did President Reagan play in the downfall of communism in the former Soviet Union and Eastern Europe? When addressing these questions and examining the pertinent evidence, even highly trained and expert historians can reach quite different conclusions.

And yet, while the interpretations of professional historians may differ, this does not suggest that all viewpoints are equally valid. Indeed, just as with any expert testimony, some arguments are more persuasive, more authoritative, more conclusive. These "stronger" arguments are often supported with more reliable data and evidence, are stated more logically and thoughtfully, and are presented more clearly, precisely, and forcefully.

This book is designed to help students become better historians—to give them the opportunity to do what historians do: examine evidence and data, weigh this evidence against what they already know, reach informed and thoughtful positions, and present and argue these positions. This is a challenging task, and most students will find it difficult. But with practice and perseverance, they can become successful historical detectives.

What students are doing here—weighing significant evidence and data to reach informed and thoughtful positions, to present and argue these positions on important questions—replicates not only what historians do, but describes what all of us as good citizens must do. Just like historians, citizens often grapple with incomplete, biased, and contradictory evidence. And, just as evidence sometimes leads historians to quite different conclusions about important historical questions, so too do citizens often disagree on questions and issues of contemporary American life. Democratic citizenship, just like history, is hardly an exact science which yields "correct" answers. Instead, it should result in reflective, informed, concerned and independent decisions from each of us.

What Is a Document-Based Question?

This book contains 22 **document-based questions**, or DBQ's. Each is an essay question that addresses a significant theme or topic in American history. You'll find that many are open-ended, posing broad questions which invite debate and will lead different students to different interpretations. Following each key question are a variety of documents. Most are primary sources, offering "eyewitness" reports from people who actually lived during the time being discussed, or who actually took part in the events being examined. These primary sources can take various forms, including diaries, letters, speeches, newspaper or magazine accounts, testimony, and reports. Other materials considered primary sources are maps, pictures, graphs, and charts. If we were examining the reason why the

Pilgrims came to Plymouth in 1620, for example, a good primary source might be *Of Plymouth Plantation*, the account of William Bradford, a leader of the Pilgrims. However, sometimes secondary sources are included as well. These are accounts reported by those who were not actually present during the event or time being described, but who have studied the primary sources and reached conclusions based on this evidence. *The Founding of New England*, a book written in 1921 by the historian James Truslow Adams, would provide a good secondary source about the motives of the Pilgrims coming to America in 1620. As you might expect, secondary sources are typically not as authoritative as primary sources can be. Remember, even two eyewitnesses to the same event can disagree about just what happened, and will often disagree about *why* it happened. Even primary sources can be flawed, biased, and invalid.

How to Use and Teach DBQ's

The document-based questions in this book can be used by teachers in a variety of ways—as independent student assignments, classroom exercises, formal student assessments, group projects, or as preparation for classroom seminars and debates, to suggest only a few. They were designed to be used after students have studied a topic or unit, so that they bring to the task some foundational knowledge and understanding of the question.

You'll find that each DBQ is followed by a brief summary and discussion of the documents, along with some grading guidelines. Three DBQ's near the beginning of the book also include sample student answers with teacher-assigned grades and comments. The first twelve DBQ's include short summary questions after each document. These are designed to help students learn to analyze and interpret documents and to focus their analysis on the question. The last ten DBQ's do not contain questions for each document. It is assumed that most students, after sufficient practice, will no longer need this extra help. Obviously, students' abilities differ. Teachers may want to stop using these questions earlier in the school year, or they may want to develop their own questions for the documents in the last ten DBQ's as well.

How much time will it take for students to carefully complete each of these DBQ's? If students have little or no previous experience with this method, you'll have to "go slow" early in the year. You might, for instance, devote two or three class periods to the first few DBQ's you do. And, you might have students do these first DBQ's in small groups—or even as a whole-class activity. As the year progresses and students become more proficient, you can shorten the process. These questions were originally designed for use with eleventh-graders. However, with practice, and when used as assessments at the end of a unit's study, able students from the ninth grade and above should be able to try their hand at this approach. Most students should be able to complete one within a 50-minute class period.

Getting Started: Guidelines for Students

The 22 **document-based questions (DBQ's)** in this book are designed to help you become a better historian and better citizen. Examining real evidence about important questions in history, then weighing evidence against what you already know in order to reach an opinion, approximates what historians do. These skills are authentic to the historical process. However, of equal importance, they are authentic to the democratic process—to what responsible citizens do in examining civic issues, formulating positions, and taking stands on these positions. Writing answers to document-based questions will help you improve your thinking skills, learn to detect biases, weigh evidence, develop logical solutions, and express yourself in clear, thoughtful, and persuasive prose. Good luck!

How to Begin

1. First of all, carefully read the question. Be sure that you know what is being asked.

2. Ask yourself: "How would I answer this question if I had no documents to examine?" Presumably you've studied the topic in class, read about it in your textbook, and, perhaps, have learned more from supplemental readings. You're not beginning the process "cold." You know a lot about the topic already, and you've probably formulated some opinions. Don't discount this knowledge. As you read the documents, build upon this preexisting understanding.

3. Before you begin to examine the documents, take a few minutes to jot down what you already know about the topic and the question. Names, dates, events, and other items that pertain to the question and topic should be included.

4. Now, after reading the question again, carefully read each document. Underline things of special importance, and write brief notes in the margin. Ask yourself: How does this document help to answer the question? What is its basic point? What biases does it contain? How credible is it? How does it change or reinforce my beliefs about the topic and question?

5. Many of the document-based questions include brief questions after each document. These questions are designed to help you focus on the main idea of the document, and to help you analyze and interpret its meaning. Provide brief, but accurate, answers to these questions. They will help you when you write your essay answer.

6. At this point, formulate a thesis statement which directly answers the question. Take a stand and state a position—one that both your preexisting knowledge and the documents support.

7. Briefly outline your essay so that you prove your thesis with supportive evidence and information *both from the documents and from knowledge you already have*. Remember, this knowledge comes from your classwork, discussions, and reading beyond the documents.

8. Carefully write your essay. Cite supporting evidence from documents within your essay in a way that strengthens and validates your thesis. Allude to these documents and other evidence in well-written, fluid prose. For instance, don't say: "As document 1 states . . . ." Instead, say: "As President Kennedy said in his inaugural address . . . ."

How Are Answers Scored? A Scoring Rubric

Here is a scoring rubric that identifies the recommended criteria used in grading DBQ essay answers. You might want to try to grade some of your own answers, or answers written by classmates. And, you might ask your teacher to duplicate one or two of the best answers in your class so that everyone can see examples of good DBQ essays.

5   Strong thesis—responds directly to the question.
    Uses documents completely and accurately; weighs the importance and
        validity of evidence.
    Cites considerable relevant information from outside learning.
    Displays a thorough understanding of the topic and related issues.
    Well structured, well written; proper spelling, grammar, mechanics.

4   Thesis stated—answers the question.
    Uses documents correctly; recognizes that all evidence is not equally valid.
    Cites some relevant information from outside learning.
    Shows an understanding of the topic and related issues.
    Clearly written and coherent; some minor errors in writing.

3   Addresses the question but has weak structure and focus.
    Uses most documents correctly—simplistic analysis; does not always weigh the
        importance and validity of evidence.
    Includes little relevant information from outside learning.
    Shows basic, though simplistic, understanding of the topic and related issues.
    Weaker organization; some errors in writing detract from essay's meaning.

2   Poor focus; fails to answer the question adequately.
    Some documents used correctly; some only paraphrased or misunderstood;
        fails to recognize any difference in the validity of evidence.
    Includes little information from outside learning—what is included is irrelevant.
    Shows little understanding of the topic and related issues.
    Poorly organized; many errors in standard English.

1   Fails to address the question; confusing and unfocused.
    Fails to use documents correctly; simply paraphrased or misunderstood.
    Includes no relevant information from beyond the documents.
    Shows almost no understanding of the topic or related issues.
    Disorganized; littered with errors in standard English.

0   No thesis; no attempt to address the question.
    Ignores or misuses the documents.
    Includes no information from beyond the documents.
    Shows no understanding of the topic or related issues.
    Lacks any organization; little attempt made; blank paper.

Unit 1: The Colonial Period

DBQ 1: Immigration

Historical Context:

From the establishment of the first successful English colony at Jamestown, Virginia, in 1607, the population of the American colonies grew rapidly. By 1700 this area contained close to 300,000 people; by 1750 it contained well over one million. In 1790 the first official census of the United States counted 3,900,000. While much of this population increase came from an unusually high birthrate (families with 10 or more children were common), about half of the increase came from massive immigration.

◆ **Directions:** The following question is based on the accompanying documents (1–5) in Part A. As you analyze the documents, take into account both the source of the document and the author's point of view. Be sure to:

1. Carefully read the document-based question. Consider what you already know about this topic. How would you answer the question if you had no documents to examine?

2. Now, read each document carefully, underlining key phrases and words that address the document-based question. You may also wish to use the margin to make brief notes. Answer the questions which follow each document.

3. Based on your own knowledge and on the information found in the documents, formulate a thesis that directly answers the question.

4. Organize supportive and relevant information into a brief outline.

5. Write a well-organized essay proving your thesis. The essay should be logically presented and should include information both from the documents and from your own knowledge outside of the documents.

> **Question:** *Why did so many people move to colonial America?*

◆ **Part A:** The following documents will help you understand the various reasons for immigration to the American colonies. Examine each document carefully, and answer the question or questions that follow.

Document 1

This is an excerpt from Olaudah Equiano's *The Interesting Narrative of the Life of Olaudah Equiano, or Gustavus Vassa, the African* (New York, 1791, vol. 1). Equiano was an African who was sold into slavery in America in the mid-1700's.

> I loved my family, I loved my village, and I especially loved my mother because I was the youngest son and I was her favorite . . . I was very happy. But my happiness ended suddenly when I was eleven [and sold into slavery. After being marched to the seacoast] the first object which saluted my eyes . . . was a slave ship. . . . I was put down under the decks.

(continued)

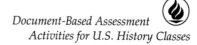

Document-Based Assessment
Activities for U.S. History Classes

DBQ 1: Immigration *(continued)*

After a long and terrible voyage, the ship came to America, where Equiano was sold into slavery. Why did Equiano and thousands of other Africans come to America during the colonial era?

_____

_____

Document 2

This excerpt is from William Penn's "Some Account of the Province of Pennsylvania in America." Written in the late 1600's, this was Penn's appeal for immigrants.

> . . . industrious farmers and day laborers . . . people who work with their hands . . . their labor will be worth more than it is in England and their living will be cheaper.

Why would land (living) be cheaper in Pennsylvania than in England? _____

_____

Why would wages for labor be higher in Pennsylvania than in England? _____

_____

What kinds of people would be likely to emigrate to Pennsylvania colony by Penn's

appeal? _____

_____

Document 3

This excerpt is from Clarence Ver Steeg's *The Formative Years, 1607–1763* (Hill and Wang, New York, 1964). Dr. Ver Steeg was a professor of history at Northwestern University. Here he explains why the English authorities of the seventeenth century encouraged emigration to the American colonies.

> . . . political economists of the period [concluded] that England was overpopulated, an assumption resulting from a theory that exportation of people to the colonies was a national asset. . . . Coupled with the theory was the fact: thousands of Englishmen were forced off the land and unwelcome itinerants became a common sight in [English cities], constituting a problem. . . .

Why did the English government promote the "exportation" of people to the American

colonies? _____

_____

What kind of people did they "export?" _____

_____

(continued)

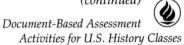

2

Document-Based Assessment
Activities for U.S. History Classes

DBQ 1: Immigration (continued)

Document 4

This excerpt is from John Winthrop's 1630 sermon "A Model of Christian Charity." Winthrop was the leader of a large group of English Puritans. He gave this address to his followers while still on board the ship *Arabella* in preparation for landing in the new colony on Massachusetts Bay. Here he speaks of what he believed was their primary motive for settlement.

> The end is to do more service to the Lord . . . that ourselves and posterity may be the better preserved from the common corruptions of this evil world to serve the Lord and work out our salvation under the power and purity of his holy ordinances.

According to Winthrop, why did the Puritans come to New England? _____

_____

Document 5

This excerpt is from James Truslow Adams' book *The Founding of New England*, published in 1919 (Little, Brown and Company, 1921, 1949; pp. 121–122). This book won the Pulitzer Prize for history in 1922. In the following excerpt, Adams is writing of the early migration to Massachusetts.

> They came for the simple reason that they wanted to better their condition. They wanted to be rid of the growing and incalculable exactions [oppressive demands] of government. They wanted to own land; and it was this last motive, perhaps, which mainly had attracted those twelve thousand persons out of sixteen thousand who swelled the population of Massachusetts in 1640, but were not church members. . . .

According to Adams, what was the primary motive for immigration to colonial New England? _____

_____

Does this document disprove what Winthrop said in Document 4? _____

_____

◆ Part B—Essay

> *Why did so many people move to colonial America?*

Grading Key

Document 1

Equiano and thousands of other Africans were forcibly brought to America as slaves.

Document 2

Many people came to Pennsylvania (and other colonies) simply to better themselves economically. Its abundance made land cheap in America, and wages were higher than in England because of the scarcity of labor.

Document 3

This secondary source explains that England, during the time of America's colonization, was seeing large numbers of poor peasants forced off the land and moving to the cities. These homeless masses became a problem for English authorities. A solution was to send England's poor to the American colonies. Some students may point out that many came as indentured servants.

Document 4

Winthrop described why the Puritans came to New England: to create a Calvinist society free from the "corruptions of this evil world."

Document 5

This secondary source points out that many Englishmen came to colonial New England for nonreligious reasons: for cheap land, to escape the "exactions of government" (taxes, conscription, injustices), to "better their condition."

Additional Information Beyond the Documents

The documents provide students with only fragments of evidence. Answers should include relevant information from beyond just the documents—information that students have learned from their classroom study. The following list suggests some of the concepts, people, and events that students could include in their essays from their outside learning.

Native Americans	Dutch in New York	patroon plan
Virginia's headright system	religious persecution	James Oglethorpe
Scots-Irish frontiersmen	Spanish and French threats	tobacco
Maryland Catholic Haven	Lord Baltimore	English Civil War
plantations	Protestant Reformation	Calvinism
enclosure movement	indentured servants	Roger Williams
farming, fishing, lumber, shipping	Pennsylvania "Dutch"	Quakers

Sample Student Essay and Suggested Grading

America was a newly discovered land that attracted many European immigrants in the 1600's. A majority of these immigrants came from England and Ireland. Many reasons contributed to this sudden immigration. Many Europeans were looking for better economic, political, and social opportunities, and they felt and hoped that America was their dream land.

In the beginning, these dreams were easily achieved. The main reason for immigration from England was the scarcity and expense of land in England. America was a vast territory of untamed land which was fresh and fertile. While a small piece of land in England was impossibly expensive, there was an abundant amount of cheap land here. Another reason for economically-related immigration was the enclosure movement in England. This granted large estate owners the right to boot out a part of the population living on their lands. This large population had nowhere else to go so they were sent to America.

Social and political freedom also played an important role in European immigration to America. John Winthrop gathered his fellow religious worshipers and led them to America where they would be free of religious persecution. In Massachusetts Winthrop and his followers established their own Puritan society, but they would not allow religious freedom for others. Many immigrants also settled in Pennsylvania because William Penn had promised religious freedom to all. Scots-Irish were another group of worshipers whose religious freedom was being persecuted in Northern Ireland by Catholics. When they settled in America, they became farmers and began their own communities along the frontier.

A totally different form of immigration was involuntary. In England General James Oglethorpe suggested that the government send a colony of debtors and criminals to Georgia to act as a buffer between Spanish Florida and South Carolina, which was rich and valuable. Oglethorpe's suggestion was for the benefit of England's economy. Poor, landless peasants in overcrowded English cities were also sent to America either voluntarily or involuntarily as indentured servants. The largest population of involuntary immigrants were slaves from Africa. In early colonial America thousands of men, women, and children were rudely kidnapped from their families so there would be cheap labor on American plantations. (Documents 1, 2, 3)

There was a great deal of attraction to America in the 1600s. Europeans hoped to achieve economic, political, and social prosperity. Immigrants hoped America would be their dream land, and to many it was.

Teacher Comments

Based on the scoring rubric, this is a good student essay—a strong 4 or a weak 5. It is well organized, directly answers the question, and is well written. It uses all of the documents (though they could be cited or alluded to more clearly) as well as relevant information from beyond the documents (enclosure movement, Scots-Irish, Oglethorpe's Georgia, etc.). While this is not a sophisticated analysis and discussion of colonial immigration, and though there are some minor historical errors, it is a quite good student essay. It was written by an eleventh-grader in 45 minutes.

Name_____ Date_____

Unit 1: The Colonial Period

DBQ 2: Economic Opportunities

Historical Context:

By the mid-eighteenth century the thirteen American colonies, which were later to become the United States, contained well over one million inhabitants. The vast number of colonial Americans made their livings as farmers. But differing climates, geography, and social practices made for great variation in the nature of work in different regions and in the level of economic success enjoyed by different American colonists.

◆ **Directions:** The following question is based on the accompanying documents (1–6). As you analyze the documents, take into account both the source of the document and the author's point of view. Be sure to:

1. Carefully read the document-based question. Consider what you already know about this topic. How would you answer the question if you had no documents to examine?

2. Now, read each document carefully, underlining key phrases and words that address the document-based question. You may also wish to use the margin to make brief notes. Answer the questions which follow each document.

3. Based on your own knowledge and on the information found in the documents, formulate a thesis that directly answers the question.

4. Organize supportive and relevant information into a brief outline.

5. Write a well-organized essay proving your thesis. The essay should be logically presented and should include information both from the documents and from your own knowledge outside of the documents.

> **Question:** *Americans often pride themselves that theirs is a "land of opportunity." How much economic opportunity truly did exist in colonial America, and what factors affected the colonists' opportunities to succeed?*

◆ **Part A:** The following documents deal with the types and extent of economic opportunities that existed in colonial America. Examine each document carefully, and answer the question or questions that follow.

Document 1

This is an excerpt from a popular college textbook explaining the causes of Bacon's Rebellion of 1676. *Colonial America* was written by Oscar T. Barck, Jr., and Hugh Talmadge Lefler, and published by Macmillan Company (1967, p. 209).

> . . . Bacon's Rebellion . . . was the first instance in the colonies "in which the common people rose not only against the royal governor, but also the rule of the privileged class."

How does this document help to address the question of this DBQ? _____
_____

(continued)

DBQ 2: Economic Opportunities *(continued)*

Document 2

This excerpt is from *An Account of Pennsylvania . . .* (1698) by Gabriel Thomas. Thomas was a Welsh Quaker who settled in Pennsylvania in the 1680's.

> . . . poor people (both men and women) of all kinds, can here get three times the wages for their labor they can in England or Wales.

What factors might help explain why wage rates were so much higher in the American

colonies than in England and Wales? _____

_____

_____

Document 3

This excerpt is from Gottlieb Mittelberger, *Journey to Pennsylvania* (1754), taken from the Harvard University edition of 1960, Oscar Handlin, editor. Mittelberger was a German schoolteacher who traveled to Pennsylvania in the early 1750's.

> [Speaking of indentured servants] Many parents in order to pay their fares in this way . . . must barter and sell their children as if they were cattle. . . . No one in this country can run away from a master who has treated him harshly and get far. . . . Our Europeans who have been purchased must work hard all of the time. . . . Thus let him . . . who can do this by manual labor in his native country stay THERE rather than come to America.

Was America "a land of opportunity" for indentured servants? _____

Explain. _____

_____

_____

_____

Can both Documents 2 and 3 be valid, or do they contradict each other? _____

_____

(continued)

Document-Based Assessment Activities for U.S. History Classes

DBQ 2: Economic Opportunities *(continued)*

Document 4

These excerpts are from Andrew Burnaby, *Travels Through the Middle Settlements in North America* (1775). Burnaby was a young Englishman who traveled through the American colonies in the years just before the American Revolution.

> The trade of this colony [Virginia] is large and extensive. Tobacco is the principal article of it. . . . Their manufactures are very inconsiderable.
>
> Boston . . . in New England, is one of the largest and most flourishing towns in North America . . . it is supposed to contain 3000 houses, and 18 or 20,000 inhabitants. . . . The buildings are in general good; the streets open and spacious . . . and the whole has much the air of some of our best country towns in England. The country round about it is exceedingly delightful.

What view does Burnaby give you of the level of economic opportunities in colonial

America? _____

_____

_____

Document 5

This excerpt is from Thomas Anburey, *Travels Through the Interior Parts of America* (1778). Anburey was a British officer during the American Revolution who, as a prisoner of war, was marched from Boston to Charlottesville, Virginia. He published his observations of America after returning to England.

> [In Virginia] It is the poor Negroes who alone work hard, and I am sorry to say, fare hard. Incredible is the fatigue which the poor wretches undergo.

What might make you suspect an anti-American bias in Document 5? _____

_____

Should we reject the validity of Anburey's statement? _____

(continued)

DBQ 2: Economic Opportunities *(continued)*

Document 6

These excerpts are from St. Jean de Crèvecoeur, "Letters From An American Farmer" (1782). Michel-Guillaume St. Jean de Crèvecoeur was a Frenchman who lived in New York from 1764 until 1780. His "Letters" grew from his travels in New York and Pennsylvania.

> What then is the American, this new man?
>
> . . . He does not find, as in Europe, a crowded society, where every place is over-stocked. There is room for every body in America. . . .
>
> The rich stay in Europe, it is only the middling and poor that emigrate.
>
> Here the rewards of his industry follow with equal steps the progress of his labor.
>
> Some few towns excepted, we are all tillers of the earth, from Nova Scotia to West Florida.

What view does Crèvecoeur give us of the extent and types of economic opportunities that

existed in colonial America? _____

_____

_____

Why were most American colonists "tillers of the earth"? _____

_____

_____

◆ **Part B—Essay**

> *Americans often pride themselves that theirs is a "land of opportunity." How much economic opportunity truly did exist in colonial America, and what factors affected the colonists' opportunities to succeed?*

9

Grading Key

Document 1

Bacon's Rebellion arose (at least in part) from resentment of the common folk against the royal governor and the powerful, privileged class. This suggests that, at least in Virginia, social injustices and inequities thwarted the opportunities of the common people.

Document 2

Wage rates in the American colonies were "three times" as high as in England and Wales, suggesting that the colonies offered great opportunities for poor men and women.

Document 3

Indentured servants had terrible lives; they were treated badly and worked very hard, with no opportunities. Mittelberger advised European workers: Stay home!

Document 4

Burnaby reported that Boston was a prosperous and delightful city. In Virginia, the major product was tobacco; few manufactured goods were produced.

Document 5

This British officer (a prisoner of war during the Revolutionary War) pointed out what terrible lives the Virginia slaves had.

Document 6

Crèvecoeur said a number of pertinent things: The "room" in America was a source of opportunity; most Americans were among Europe's poor and came here seeking opportunities; virtually all colonists were farmers; hard work had its rewards.

Additional Information Beyond the Documents

The documents provide students with only fragments of evidence. Answers should include relevant information from beyond just the documents—information that students have learned from their classroom study. The following list suggests some of the concepts and events that students could use in their essays from their outside learning.

class structures of different colonial regions	public education	indentured servitude
	headright system	tidewater aristocracy
slavery	farming—by regions	primogeniture
land ownership	New York Dutch patroons	labor shortage
triangular trade	declining New England soil	social deference

Unit 2: Revolution, Confederation, Constitution

DBQ 3: Causes of the Revolutionary War

Historical Context:

1763 marked the end of the French and Indian War, the final defeat of the French and their Native American allies in America. For America's English colonists, this was a cause for great celebration and pride in their English identity. Expressions of English patriotism were widespread. But only twelve years later, these same American colonists found themselves locked in a bitter and violent conflict with the mother country that had so recently been the object of their proud respect. To this day, now over two hundred years later, the reasons behind this abrupt transition of England and her American colonies from allies to enemies are debated.

◆ **Directions:** The following question is based on the accompanying documents (1–7). As you analyze the documents, take into account both the source of the document and the author's point of view. Be sure to:

1. Carefully read the document-based question. Consider what you already know about this topic. How would you answer the question if you had no documents to examine?

2. Now, read each document carefully, underlining key phrases and words that address the document-based question. You may also wish to use the margin to make brief notes. Answer the questions which follow each document.

3. Based on your own knowledge and on the information found in the documents, formulate a thesis that directly answers the question.

4. Organize supportive and relevant information into a brief outline.

5. Write a well-organized essay proving your thesis. The essay should be logically presented and should include information both from the documents and from your own knowledge outside of the documents.

Question: *Were the American colonists justified in waging war and breaking away from Britain?*

◆ **Part A:** The following documents address the question of whether the American colonists were really justified in waging war against England. Examine each document carefully, and answer the question or questions that follow.

Document 1

This excerpt is from "Considerations . . .," a pamphlet written by Thomas Whately. Whately was an advisor to George Grenville, British Chancellor of the Exchequer (1763–1765) and the author of the Stamp Act. In this pamphlet, Whately explained why the British were justified in levying taxes on their American colonists.

> We are not yet recovered from a War undertaken solely for their [the Americans'] Protection . . . a War undertaken for their defense only . . . they should contribute to the Preservation of the Advantages they have received. . . .

Why did Whately (and probably most other English officials) feel that the American colonists should be willing to pay higher taxes to Parliament? _____

_____

(continued)

DBQ 3: Causes of the Revolutionary War (continued)

Document 2

These excerpts are from *Letters From a Farmer in Pennsylvania*, [1767–1768] by John Dickinson. Dickinson was a Pennsylvania political leader who served in the Stamp Act Congress of 1765. Later in his career, he served in the Continental Congress, and later still, in the Constitutional Convention. In the following statement, Dickinson condemned some of the new taxes being imposed by Parliament.

> There is another late act of parliament, which appears to me to be unconstitutional, and . . . destructive to the liberty of these colonies. . . .
>
> The parliament unquestionably possesses a legal authority to regulate the trade of Great Britain, and all her colonies. I have looked over every statute [law] relating to these colonies, from their first settlement to this time; and I find every one of them founded on this principle, till the Stamp Act administration. . . . All before, are calculated to regulate trade. . . . The raising of revenue . . . was never intended. . . . Never did the British parliament, [until the passage of the Stamp Act] think of imposing duties in America for the purpose of raising a revenue.
>
> [The Townshend Acts claim the authority] to impose duties on these colonies, not for the regulation of trade . . . but for the single purpose of levying money upon us.

According to Dickinson, what taxes was Parliament justified in imposing on the colonies? _____

Why did he object to the Stamp Act and the Townshend Acts? _____

_____

Document 3

On March 5, 1770, a crowd of Boston boys and men surrounded a number of British soldiers and began taunting and cursing them while pelting them with snowballs. Order quickly broke down and the frightened soldiers fired into the crowd. When the shooting ended, several people were dead and more were wounded. This engraving by Paul Revere, a leader of the Boston Sons of Liberty, was sent throughout the colonies in the following weeks to arouse anti-British feelings. (The original is in the John Morgan Hill collection, Yale University.)

How does the engraving tell a different story from the above description of the Boston Massacre?

_____

_____

Where do you suppose the term "massacre" to describe this event came from? _____

_____

(continued)

DBQ 3: Causes of the Revolutionary War *(continued)*

Document 4

In *The Journal of Nicholas Cresswell, 1774–1777*, Cresswell, a young Englishman, kept an account of his travels through the American colonies. The following excerpts are dated October 19, 1774 and tell of his visit to Alexandria, Virginia. (From *The Journal of Nicholas Cresswell, 1774–1777*, edited by Samuel Thornely. New York: The Dial Press, Inc., 1924.)

> Everything here is in the utmost confusion. Committees are appointed to inspect into the character and conduct of every tradesman, to prevent them selling tea or buying British manufacturers. Some have been tarred and feathered, others had their property burned and destroyed by the populace.
>
> The King is openly cursed, and his authority set at defiance . . . everything is ripe for rebellion. The New Englanders by their canting, whining, insinuating tricks have persuaded the rest of the colonies that the government is going to make absolute slaves of them.

Who did Cresswell blame for the growing antagonism between the British and the

American colonists? _____

_____

Document 5

This excerpt is from "Declaration of the Causes and Necessity of Taking up Arms," issued by the Second Continental Congress on July 5, 1775. The war had broken out in April, when British forces had marched to Lexington and Concord, two villages just outside of Boston. This document, written largely by John Dickinson and Thomas Jefferson, was designed to explain and justify the fighting that had continued since April.

> [The British declare] that parliament can "of right make laws to bind us in all cases whatsoever." What is to defend us against so enormous, so unlimited a power? . . . We are reduced to the alternative of choosing an unconditional submission to the tyranny of irritated [British officials], or resistance by force.— The latter is our choice.

Why, according to this document, were the Americans justified in fighting the British?

_____

_____

_____

(continued)

DBQ 3: Causes of the Revolutionary War (continued)

Document 6

These excerpts are from Thomas Paine's "Common Sense," published in January 1776. This popular pamphlet helped to convince many Americans that the conflict with England was beyond peaceful settlement and that independence was America's only course.

Men of passive tempers look somewhat lightly over the offenses of Great Britain, and, still hoping for the best, are apt to call out, COME, COME, WE SHALL BE FRIENDS AGAIN FOR ALL THIS. But . . . then tell me whether you can hereafter love, honour, and faithfully serve the power that hath carried fire and sword into your land?

. . . No man was a warmer wisher for a [peaceful settlement] than myself, before the fatal nineteenth of April, 1775 [the battles at Lexington and Concord, Massachusetts occurred on this day], but the moment the event of that day was made known, I rejected the hardened, sullen-tempered [King of England] for ever.

Why was Paine unwilling to be reconciled with Britain? _____
_____
Was Paine an objective and unbiased reporter? Explain. _____
_____

Document 7

These excerpts are from "The Declaration of Independence," adopted by The Continental Congress of July 4, 1776.

The history of the present King of Great Britain is a history of repeated injuries and usurpations [unlawful seizures], all having in direct object the establishment of an absolute Tyranny over these States.

In every stage of these Oppressions We have Petitioned for Redress in the most humble terms; Our repeated Petitions have been answered only by repeated injury. A Prince, whose character is thus marked by every act which may define a Tyrant, is unfit to be the ruler of a free people.

How does this document describe King George? _____
_____
Was the Declaration an objective and unbiased statement of the American-British conflict? Explain. _____
_____

◆ **Part B—Essay**

Were the colonists justified in waging war and breaking away from Britain?

Grading Key

Document 1

Whately and Grenville (and others) felt that the American colonists should gladly pay higher taxes. After all, the huge debts had been incurred "solely" for America's defense. The implication is that Americans who complained were selfish and ungrateful.

Document 2

Dickinson argued (in 1768) that the colonies acknowledged and accepted Parliament's right to "regulate the trade" of the entire British empire by imposing tariffs and other duties. But Parliament did not have the authority to levy taxes for "the purpose of raising a revenue." To allow this was "destructive to the liberty of these colonies."

Document 3

Revere's engraving was a marvelous piece of anti-British propaganda, depicting the unfortunate event as a "massacre" of peaceful Bostonians by the vile and vicious British soldiers.

Document 4

This document expressed a British bias, condemning the New Englanders for their "canting, whining, insinuating tricks" which are designed to spread unfounded anti-British propaganda to Americans in other colonies. (Students may cite Document 3 as an example of such a "trick.")

Document 5

This document was issued by the Continental Congress to justify the colonies defending themselves against British "tyranny" (since the outbreak of fighting three months earlier at Lexington and Concord). Parliament's claim that it had authority over the colonies "in all cases whatsoever" so threatened Americans' liberties that we had to resist by force.

Document 6

This is the classic statement of revolutionary sentiment, designed to convince wavering Americans that revolution and independence were the only choice.

Document 7

This, America's most sacred document from its war for independence, was designed to portray the British and King George in the very worst light, accusing Britain's "repeated injuries" of growing from the "direct object" of establishing an "absolute Tyranny" over America.

Hopefully, students will recognize and discuss the biased, propagandistic nature of many of these documents.

Additional Information Beyond the Documents

The documents provide students with only fragments of evidence. Answers should include relevant information from beyond just the documents—information that students have learned from their classroom study. The following list suggests some of the concepts, people, and events that students could include in their essays from their outside learning.

French and Indian War	Stamp Act	mercantilism
Navigation Acts	Sons of Liberty	Tories and Patriots
James Otis	virtual representation	Declaratory Act
Townshend Acts	Tea Act	Committees of Correspondence
Boston Tea Party	coercive acts	First Continental Congress
Sam Adams	Lexington and Concord	

Sample Student Essay and Suggested Grading

When the French and Indian War had ended in 1763 Americans had visions of the British packing up their guns and going home. To their dismay, Britain did just the opposite; they actually sent in more troops to tighten the imperial control and raise money to help pay for war debts. Americans were shocked. After all, they had been used to the policy of salutary neglect for many years now. An outsider from the situation could see two sides to this story. Britain, the mother country was in need of money, and looked to their overseas colony—which had been directly aided in the war. Americans felt cheated and threatened by the sudden tightening of control and, as every child does who eventually breaks away from his or her parents, rebelled. In this sense the colonists were justified in waging war and in breaking away from Britain.

In a pamphlet, "Considerations," written by Thomas Whatley, Britain's view of taxation is clearly expressed. They feel that for all of the time, effort, and money that they spent helping the colonists in the French and Indian war, the colonists should be willing to help them out and be willing to pay higher taxes. The colonists, however, saw these new taxes (as Britain imposed: ex. Sugar Act and Stamp Act) as taxes for revenue purposes only and as a threat to their rights as Englishmen. They were being taxed without representation in Parliament, and they were not being taxed for any reasons beneficial to their colonies.

Misunderstandings and frustrations grew even more when Benjamin Franklin made the mistake of saying that the colonies were opposed only to "internal" taxes. This led Parliament to impose the Townshend Acts, which raised taxes on imported goods. This, of course, was not at all okay with the colonists. When the Stamp Act Congress was formed, it did not say—we will accept external taxes, but we will not accept any taxes for revenue purposes when we remain unrepresented in Parliament.

Tensions began mounting, and in 1770 the Boston Massacre occurred. At this point the British had come to believe that the colonists were "whining and insinuating" (from the journal of N. Cresswell). Britain thought that the colonies were reacting brashly and unthoughtfully. The colonists were merely fighting for their rights as Englishmen. When the Tea Act was passed allowing the British East India Company to sell tea cheaply in the Boston Port, rebellion broke loose. The famous Boston Tea Party was performed by the angry Sons of Liberty as they unloaded British tea in the harbor. Now England was absolutely furious, and quite frankly the colonists were ready to rub it in their face. When, on April, 1775 it was discovered that New England had been hiding war materials, fighting broke out at Lexington and Concord.

This was a turning point. It was now that people like Thomas Paine could never turn back and forgive Britain. He writes in "Common Sense," "I rejected the hard, sullen tempered king forever." It wasn't until a year later, when the Declaration of Independence was declared in 1776 that the war cry changed to a battle for independence.

In the previous decade, through a series of misunderstandings, Britain had imposed acts upon the colonists to tighten their power. Angered and frustrated, the colonists fought back in every way possible. Britain, unfortunately, reacted by only tightening their control even more. At this point Americans had to ask themselves a question; they answered this question by declaring a war. They were stepping up initially to defend themselves against an imposing power, and rightfully so. They then took the next step—independence.

Teacher Comments

This is a good student essay, certainly a 4, possibly a weak 5. It was well written, stated and defended a firm thesis, used most documents accurately, included some relevant information from beyond the documents (the mention of Franklin's testimony to Parliament about the Stamp Act was especially impressive), and displayed a solid understanding of the topic and related issues. The student did omit some pertinent information (the Intolerable Acts, for instance), some documents deserved more discussion (Revere's engraving and the propaganda of the Sons of Liberty, for instance), and the entire essay was lacking somewhat in its understanding and consideration of biases. Still, it's a good job, especially so for an eleventh-grader. The student devoted 15 minutes to part A, 45 minutes to part B (the essay).

Unit 2: Revolution, Confederation, Constitution

DBQ 4: Ratifying the Constitution

Historical Context:

Today, over 200 years after it was written and ratified, most Americans think of the U.S. Constitution as something almost sacred. We assume that this great document has always been honored and revered. This is not true. When it was written in 1787 and submitted to the states for ratification, it set off months of fierce and often bitter debate. There were, of course, many who welcomed it as a stronger and more effective national government which could successfully tie the 13 states together into a common nation. But others were fearful of this proposed powerful new national government. Only a few years earlier they had fought a war against a too powerful, distant central government. Why should they now erect a new distant central government which could threaten their liberties just as King George and Parliament had? The debate went on in towns and villages across the country for months. Some of the smaller states ratified the new Constitution quickly, but in most states the debate continued. In February of 1788, the Massachusetts convention voted 187 to 168 to ratify the Constitution. In June, Virginia ratified, 89 to 79. New York followed almost immediately. Now, with the approval of 11 states, the new government was established. In April of 1789 George Washington was inaugurated President, even though two states still had not approved the Constitution. It took North Carolina until November 1789 and Rhode Island until May 1790 to join the new government.

◆ **Directions:** The following question is based on the accompanying documents (1–6). As you analyze the documents, take into account both the source of the document and the author's point of view. Be sure to:

1. Carefully read the document-based question. Consider what you already know about this topic. How would you answer the question if you had no documents to examine?

2. Now, read each document carefully, underlining key phrases and words that address the document-based question. You may also wish to use the margin to make brief notes. Answer the questions which follow each document.

3. Based on your own knowledge and on the information found in the documents, formulate a thesis that directly answers the question.

4. Organize supportive and relevant information into a brief outline.

5. Write a well-organized essay proving your thesis. The essay should be logically presented and should include information both from the documents and from your own knowledge outside of the documents.

> **Question:** *What were the major arguments used by each side (the supporters and the opponents) in the debates over the ratification of the U.S. Constitution?*

◆ **Part A:** The following documents address various arguments made in support of, or in opposition to, ratifying the U.S. Constitution. Examine each document carefully, and answer the question or questions that follow.

(continued)

DBQ 4: Ratifying the Constitution *(continued)*

Document 1

This excerpt is from a newspaper, *The Massachusetts Sentinel*, October 20, 1787. (From *Voices of America: Readings in American History*, Thomas R. Frazier, ed. Boston: Houghton Mifflin, 1985, p. 61.)

> Let us look and behold the distresses which prevail in every part of our country . . . the complaints of our farmers . . . the complaints of every class of public creditors . . . the melancholy faces of our working people . . . our ships rotting in our harbors . . . the insults that are offered to the American name and character in every court of Europe. . . . View these things, fellow citizens, and then say that we do not require a new, a protecting, and efficient federal government if you can.

Why does the editor of this newspaper support ratifying the Constitution?

_____

_____

_____

Document 2

This excerpt is from "Observations on the New Federal Constitution and on the Federal and State Conventions," by Mercy Otis Warren. It originally appeared as a newspaper article in the spring of 1788.

> There is no security in the system [under the proposed new U.S. Constitution] either for the rights of conscience or the liberty of the press. . . . The executive and the legislat[ure] are so dangerously blended that they give just cause for alarm. . . . There is no provision for a rotation nor anything else to prevent a political office from remaining in the same hands for life.

Why did Mercy Otis Warren oppose ratifying the Constitution? _____

_____

_____

_____

(continued)

DBQ 4: Ratifying the Constitution *(continued)*

Document 3

These excerpts are from a letter written by George Washington to John Jay, dated August 1, 1786. In these lines, Washington is agreeing with Jay's criticism of the Articles of Confederation.

> Your sentiments, that our affairs are drawing rapidly to a crisis, accord with my own. . . .
> We have errors to correct. We have probably had too good an opinion of human nature
> in forming our confederation . . .
>
> . . . thirteeen sovereign, independent, disunited States are in the habit of . . . refusing
> compliance with [our national Congress] at their option.
>
> Would to God, that wise measures may be taken in time to avert the consequences we have
> but too much reason to apprehend. . . .

What did Washington mean by saying "we have errors to correct?" _____

_____

What do you suppose he meant by saying "we have probably had too good an opinion of

human nature in forming our confederation? _____

_____

_____

Document 4

This excerpt is from a speech by Patrick Henry, a delegate to the Virginia State Constitutional Ratification Convention, given in June 1788. (From Jonathan Elliot, ed., *The Debates in the Several State Conventions on the Adoption of the Federal Constitution*. Philadelphia: Lippincott, 1836.)

> . . . Here is a resolution as radical as that which separated us from Great Britain. It is radical
> in this transition; our rights and privileges are endangered, and the sovereignty of the states
> will be relinquished. . . . The rights of conscience, trial by jury, liberty of the press . . . are
> rendered insecure.

Why did Patrick Henry oppose the Constitution? _____

_____

_____

(continued)

19
*Document-Based Assessment
Activities for U.S. History Classes*

DBQ 4: Ratifying the Constitution *(continued)*

Document 5

This excerpt is from a speech by Amos Singletree, member of the Massachusetts Constitutional Ratification Convention, given in January 1788. (From Jonathan Elliot, ed., *The Debates in the Several State Conventions on the Adoption of the Federal Constitution*, Philadelphia: Lippincott, 1836.)

> These lawyers and men of learning, and monied men, that talk so finely and gloss over matters so smoothly, to make us poor illiterate people swallow down the pill, expect to get into Congress themselves . . . and get all the power and all the money into their own hands, and then they will swallow all us little folks . . .

Why did Amos Singletree oppose the Constitution? _____

_____

Document 6

This excerpt is from a resolution from the Massachusetts Constitutional Ratification Convention, February 1788. This Convention approved the Constitution with a vote of 187 to 168. (From Jonathan Elliot, ed., *The Debates in the Several State Conventions on the Adoption of the Federal Constitution*, Philadelphia: Lippincott, 1836.)

> . . . it is the opinion of this Convention that certain amendments and alterations in the said Constitution would remove the fears and quiet the apprehensions of many of the good people of the commonwealth *[the resolution goes on to recommend such amendments as]* . . . that all powers not expressly delegated by the . . . Constitution are reserved to the several states . . . that no person be tried for any crime . . . until he be first indicted by a grand jury . . .

What addition to the U.S. Constitution was suggested as a way to win the approval of

many of its opponents? _____

_____

◆ Part B—Essay

What were the major arguments used by each side (the supporters and the opponents) in the debates over the ratification of the U.S. Constitution?

Grading Key

Document 1

This newspaper editorial advocated that the United States adopt a new federal constitution—one that could give us a stronger, more efficient federal government, one that would strengthen our international trade, help our farmers, maintain a sound currency, and protect the American name and character.

Document 2

Mercy Otis Warren opposed the new Constitution, fearing that it would threaten our "rights of conscience" and "liberty of the press," and create a dangerously powerful national government. She was alarmed at how the executive and legislature were "dangerously blended."

Document 3

Washington agreed with Jay that the Articles had "errors" that needed to be corrected. He complained that, as it was, the thirteen "disunited States" could never agree. He also suggested that human nature being what it was, America needed a stronger (that is, less democratic) national government.

Document 4

Patrick Henry strongly opposed the new U.S. Constitution. Just like Mercy Otis Warren, he feared that it would endanger our individual rights, and that it would force the states to abandon their "sovereignty."

Document 5

Amos Singletree was a farmer who opposed Massachusetts ratifying the new U.S. Constitution. He, like many poorer and less educated Americans, feared that the new Constitution would be used by the "lawyers and men of learning, and monied men" to "get all the power and all the money into their own hands."

Document 6

Though the Massachusetts Constitutional Ratification Convention approved the U.S. Constitution, it recommended the addition of "certain amendments" that would protect the rights of people and of the states. This recommendation (and similar ones made by other state ratification conventions) led to the later adoption of the Bill of Rights.

Additional Information Beyond the Documents

The documents provide students with only fragments of evidence. Answers should include relevant information from beyond just the documents—information that students have learned from their classroom study. The following list suggests some of the concepts, people, and events that students might use in their essays from their outside learning.

Articles of Confederation	states rights	Charles Beard's economic interpretation
interstate commerce problems	Shays's Rebellion	Rhode Island's currency inflation
Alexander Hamilton	postwar depression	Federalists vs. Anti-Federalists
Bill of Rights	foreign trade problems	Annapolis Convention
James Madison	compromises	Federalist Papers

Sample Student Essay and Suggested Grading

The debate over ratification of the US Constitution was an argument of democracy versus oppression, the little guy versus the big guy, the rights of individuals and states; and a reaction to the Critical Period. Each side, the Federalists and the Antifederalists, presented its case before the nation in hope of receiving its support. The shift in American attitudes, as a result of the crises of the Critical Period, perhaps determined the eventual acceptance of the Constitution. It was ratified from 1788 to 1790, but not without great effort from both sides.

By 1787, most people were not happy under the Articles of Confederation. The farmers were becoming debtors; revolts such as Shays' rebellion occurred; inflation increased at astronomical levels; and the government could do little about it. The new document, the Constitution, awaited ratification. Some argued in favor of the change because the Articles were detrimental to everyone (Document 1). The Critical Period was more than many could handle. The state of mankind was on the honor system under the Articles and it was failing miserably (Document 3) The Constitution was a reflexive action. Many felt its ratification necessary to maintain America and Americans. Conditions continued to totter until the complete ratification of the Constitution.

There were others who did not reject the Articles. They qualified their position against the Constitution in opposition to change. Some feared the Constitution was potentially oppressive and undemocratic. After all, the method of gaining federal office was hardly democratic (Document 2) The first presidents were picked by an electoral college whose votes were determined by state legislatures. US Senators were also picked by state legislatures. And Federal judges were appointed, serving for life. Indeed, the people were right to consider this as a quasi-democracy. Others, indeed, feared transition from the Articles to the Constitution; basic human rights could be diminished (Document 4) Some who of the poor and less educated feared the potential power of their affluent nemeses. "Us poor illiterate people stand no chance against the Big guys—the bankers, owners, and merchants." (Document 5) Farmers especially feared life under a strong central government, although they didn't mind a strong state government. The antifederalists emerged with an encompassing argument.

Alexander Hamilton, in reaction to this, rounded up his colleagues John Jay and James Madison to write the *Federalist Papers*. Their work, published under the pseudonym "Publius," helped to persuade NY to ratify the Constitution. They saw people's hesitation in regard to personal rights, and they promised to add a Bill of Rights. Modeled after Virginia's, the Bill not only preserved individual and states' rights, but it convinced some states to ratify the document in question (Document 6) Also, the Constitution had provisions for taxation and collection. The anti's were leery of forced taxation, but the Federalists were eager to see the government empowered. Not on the honor system this time, individual financial accountability would give the US government its much needed authority. The Federalists emerged as clear-cut supporters of the Constitution.

Both the Federalists and the Antifederalists attacked the issues that kept America down during the Critical Period. They considered personal and states' rights; the effects of a strong central government; and the principles and applications behind the Constitution itself. In the end, the Federalists prevailed but not without a strong fight from the Antifederalists.

Teacher Comments

This essay is a strong 3 or weak 4. The student stated a thesis, generally used documents correctly, cited some valuable information from beyond just the documents given, and demonstrated some understanding of the topic and its issues. The essay also was well written and organized. Nonetheless there are weaknesses. The student could have been clearer about the failures and weaknesses of the Articles of Confederation and the problems faced by the nation during the Critical Period. Some statements are vague and some allusions are obscure—for instance, the "honor system" comments in paragraphs two and four probably refer to Document 3 (Washington's point about human nature), but do so in a vague way suggesting a shallow understanding. Indeed, a tone of vagueness runs through the entire essay, suggesting a less than total grasp and mastery of the issues involved. Still, it's a pretty good job, especially for an eleventh-grader who wrote for only 45 minutes.

Unit 3: The New Nation (1789–1825)

DBQ 5: Growth of Political Parties

Historical Context:

Today, most of us associate the American political system with the ongoing conflict of political parties. Republican Party leaders and Democratic Party leaders carry on a seeming nonstop debate as they compete for the support and votes of the American public. But two hundred years ago, in the early days of the American Republic, political parties did not exist, and our early leaders were generally glad of it. Most of them, including President Washington, feared that the existence of political parties would split the young country into warring groups, undermine our fragile national unity, and weaken public suppport for the new Constitution. Yet, though Washington and others tried to resist them, political parties nonetheless began to form, and gradually developed into the party system we have today.

◆ **Directions:** The following question is based on the accompanying documents (1–7). As you analyze the documents, take into account both the source of the document and the author's point of view. Be sure to:

1. Carefully read the document-based question. Consider what you already know about this topic. How would you answer the question if you had no documents to examine?
2. Now, read each document carefully, underlining key phrases and words that address the document-based question. You may also wish to use the margin to make brief notes. Answer the questions which follow each document.
3. Based on your own knowledge and on the information found in the documents, formulate a thesis that directly answers the question.
4. Organize supportive and relevant information into a brief outline.
5. Write a well-organized essay proving your thesis. The essay should be logically presented and should include information both from the documents and from your own knowledge outside of the documents.

> **Question:** *What led to the rise of political parties in the 1790's?*

◆ **Part A:** The following documents deal with the rise of political parties during the 1790's. Examine each document carefully, and answer the question or questions that follow.

Document 1

This excerpt is from a memo written by Thomas Jefferson in 1790, but published years later.

> . . . Hamilton was not only a monarchist, but [in support] of a monarchy [based upon] corruption.

What did Jefferson think of Hamilton? _____

_____

_____

(continued)

DBQ 5: Growth of Political Parties *(continued)*

Document 2

These excerpts are from a letter written by Alexander Hamilton to a friend in 1792.

> . . . Mr. Madison, co-operating with Mr. Jefferson, is at the head of a faction, decidedly hostile to me, and my administration; and actuated [motivated] by views . . . subversive of the principles of good government, and dangerous to the Union. . . . Mr. Jefferson . . . [displays] his dislike of . . . funding [the] debt. . . . In respect to our foreign politics, the views of these gentlemen [Jefferson and his supporters] are . . . unsound, and dangerous. They have a womanish attachment to France, and a womanish resentment against Great Britain.

Why did Hamilton distrust Madison, Jefferson, and their faction (party) and feel that they were dangerous to America's government? _____

_____

_____

Document 3

This excerpt is from a letter written by Thomas Jefferson in December of 1794.

> The excise tax is an infernal [hellish] one . . . [the public's] detestation [hatred] of the excise tax is universal, and has now associated to it a detestation of the government. . . .

What did Jefferson think of Hamilton's excise tax? _____

_____

_____

Document 4

These excerpts are from "The Farewell Address," which President Washington released to the newspapers in September of 1796, six months before his retirement from the presidency. The primary purpose of this "farewell" was to announce his decision not to run for a third term as president. But Washington also saw it as an opportunity to provide some valuable advice to the American people.

> Let me . . . warn you in the most solemn manner against the baneful [evil] effects of the spirit of party. . . . It serves always to distract the public councils and enfeeble the public administration. It agitates the community with ill-founded jealousies and false alarms; kindles the animosity of one part against another; foments [stirs up] . . . riot and insurrection [rebellion].

Why did Washington oppose political parties? _____

_____

From your viewpoint, two centuries later, do you agree with Washington's warning? Explain.

_____

_____

(continued)

DBQ 5: Growth of Political Parties *(continued)*

Document 5

This excerpt is from a letter from Vice President Thomas Jefferson to John Wise in 1798.

> Two political Sects [parties] have arisen within the United States; the one . . . called Federalists, sometimes Aristocrats or monocrats & sometimes Tories . . . the [other] are . . . republicans, whigs . . .

What did Jefferson think of Hamilton's political sect? _____

_____

Document 6

This excerpt is from a statement by Federalist Congressman John Allen, of Connecticut, in support of the Sedition Act of 1798. (From *Annals of Congress*, Fifth Congress, Second Session, July 5, 1798.)

> If ever there was a nation which required a law of this kind, it is this. . . . look at certain papers printed in this city and elsewhere [which print] the most shameless falsehoods against the representatives of the people. . . . The freedom of the press and opinions was never understood to give the right of publishing falsehoods and slanders, nor of exciting sedition, insurrection, and slaughter. . . .

How did Congressman Allen defend the Sedition Act? _____

_____

How do you suppose Jefferson, Madison, and their supporters viewed this law? _____

_____

Document 7

This excerpt is from *An Essay on the Liberty of the Press*, by George Hay (Philadelphia, 1799). Hay was a member of the Virginia State Legislature.

> The freedom of the press . . . means the total exemption of the press from any kind of legislative control, and consequently the Sedition Bill . . . is an abridgement [reduction] of its liberty, and expressly forbidden by the constitution.

Do you suppose that Hay was a Federalist, or a supporter of Jefferson? What makes you believe this? _____

_____

◆ **Part B—Essay**

> *What led to the rise of political parties in the 1790's?*

Grading Key

Document 1

Jefferson considered Hamilton and his supporters corrupt "monarchists."

Document 2

Hamilton believed that Jefferson, Madison, and their supporters were opposed to him (They were!), a threat to good government, and dangerous to the nation. He condemned them for their opposition to funding the national debt and for their support of France and opposition to Britain.

Document 3

Here Jefferson condemned another part of Hamilton's financial plan—the excise tax.

Document 4

Washington warned against the evil influence of political parties, believing that parties would stir up rebellions by pitting one group of Americans against another.

Document 5

Jefferson admitted that there existed two parties: his, made up of Republicans, and the Federalists, a group of aristocrats, monarchists, and tories.

Document 6

This Federalist Congressman supported the Sedition Act, suggesting that "freedom of speech" was being used by Jefferson's supporters to slander President Adams' administration.

Document 7

Hay opposed the Sedition Bill, believing it to be a violation of "freedom of speech." Presumably, he was a Jeffersonian.

Additional Information Beyond the Documents

The documents provide students with only fragments of evidence. Answers should include relevant information from beyond just the documents—information that students have learned from their classroom study. The following list suggests some of the concepts, people, and events that students could include in their essays from their outside learning.

Bill of Rights	Hamilton's financial plan	Bank of the U.S.
funding the National Debt	assuming states' debts	French Revolution
Neutrality Act	citizen Genet	Jay's Treaty
Whiskey Rebellion	John Adams	XYZ Affair
Alien Act	Virginia and Kentucky Resolutions	

Unit 3: The New Nation (1789–1825)

DBQ 6: The War of 1812

Historical Context:

In 1812, only 29 years after the American Revolution, the United States found itself again at war with Great Britain. The threat of war had been brewing for some time, and this War of 1812 was not unexpected. Since the 1790's, America's leaders had tried to avoid being drawn into a series of wars between France and Britain. In 1793 President Washington issued a proclamation of neutrality asking his countrymen to be impartial toward both Britain and France. In 1800 President Adams agreed to the Convention of 1800. This ended the alliance America had formed with France during the American Revolution, an alliance which now threatened to draw America into Europe's wars. Following Adams, President Jefferson continued to steer clear of war with France and Britain. However, when both countries violated American trading rights, with Britain often stopping American ships, seizing cargoes, and kidnapping sailors (a practice called "impressment"), Jefferson called for a total embargo (or ban) on American trading. Unfortunately, this "Embargo of 1807" failed to force the European powers to respect our rights, and severely harmed our own economy, throwing thousands of merchants, shippers, and sailors out of work. When James Madison became president in 1809, he found himself facing the same problem: How could we force Britain and France to respect our rights on the high seas without being forced to war? Finally, after three years of failed diplomatic efforts, Madison asked Congress to declare war on Great Britain.

◆ **Directions:** The following question is based on the accompanying documents (1–8). As you analyze the documents, take into account both the source of the document and the author's point of view. Be sure to:

1. Carefully read the document-based question. Consider what you already know about this topic. How would you answer the question if you had no documents to examine?

2. Now, read each document carefully, underlining key phrases and words that address the document-based question. You may also wish to use the margin to make brief notes. Answer the questions which follow each document.

3. Based on your own knowledge and on the information found in the documents, formulate a thesis that directly answers the question.

4. Organize supportive and relevant information into a brief outline.

5. Write a well-organized essay proving your thesis. The essay should be logically presented and should include information both from the documents and from your own knowledge outside of the documents.

> **Question:** *What forces led Americans to declare war on Britain in 1812?*

◆ **Part A:** The following documents address the factors that led America into war with Britain in 1812. Examine each document carefully, and answer the question or questions that follow.

(continued)

DBQ 6: The War of 1812 *(continued)*

Document 1

In November 1811, the Committee on Foreign Relations of the U.S. House of Representatives reported on our nation's growing conflict with France and Britain. In the following excerpt, the report explains our complaints against Britain. (From *Annals of the Congress of the United States*, Twelfth Congress.)

> To sum up, in a word, the great causes of complaint against Great Britain, your committee need only say, that the United States, as a sovereign and independent Power, claim the right to use the ocean, which is the common and acknowledged highway of nations, for the purposes of transporting, in their own vessels, the products of their own soil and the acquisitions of their own industry. . . . Great Britain, in defiance of this incontestable [clear and certain] right, captures every American vessel bound to, or returning from, a port where her commerce is not favored; enslaves our seamen, and in spite of our [complaints and protests], perseveres in these aggressions.

According to this congressional report, what was America's major complaint against Great Britain? _____

_____

_____

Document 2

This excerpt is from a speech made by Congressman John C. Calhoun, a Democratic-Republican member of the House of Representatives from South Carolina. Calhoun gave this address on December 12, 1811, six months before war was declared on Britain—but at this time, he clearly foresaw the threat of war. (From *The Debates and Proceedings in the Congress of the United States, First to Eighteenth Congress*, Vol. 23.)

> The question . . . is reduced to this single point—which shall we do, abandon or defend our own commercial and maritime rights, and the personal liberties of our citizens employed in exercising them? These rights are essentially attacked, and war is the only means of redress. . . . I know of one principle to make a nation great . . . and that is to protect every citizen in the lawful pursuit of his business. . . . Protection and patriotism are reciprocal . . . if [the British] persist in such daring insult and injury to [the United States], it will be bound in honor and interest to resist.

How does this statement by Congressman Calhoun support Document 1? _____

_____

_____

(continued)

DBQ 6: The War of 1812 (continued)

Document 3

This excerpt is from a speech by Congressman John Randolph of Virginia, given in the House of Representatives on December 16, 1811. (From *Annals of Congress*, Twelfth Congress.)

> . . . if you go to war it will not be for the protection of . . . maritime rights. Gentlemen from the North have been taken up to some high mountain and shown all the kingdoms of the earth; and Canada seems tempting in their sight. . . . Agrarian cupidity [greed for farm land], not maritime right, urges the war.

What did Congressman Randolph believe was "really" behind the talk about war with England?

_____

_____

_____

Document 4

These excerpts from President Madison's Declaration of War were read to Congress on June 1, 1812.

> We behold our seafaring citizens still the daily victims of lawless violence. . . . We behold our vessels . . . wrested [taken] from their lawful destinations . . . in [to] British ports. . . . We behold, in fine, on the side of Great Britain a state of war against the United States . . .

According to this excerpt from President Madison's Declaration of War, what seemed to be the

primary reason for the War of 1812? _____

_____

_____

_____

(continued)

29   *Document-Based Assessment
Activities for U.S. History Classes*

DBQ 6: The War of 1812 *(continued)*

Document 5

The U.S. House of Representatives vote for war, June 4, 1812.

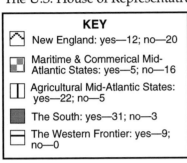

KEY
- New England: yes—12; no—20
- Maritime & Commerical Mid-Atlantic States: yes—5; no—16
- Agricultural Mid-Atlantic States: yes—22; no—5
- The South: yes—31; no—3
- The Western Frontier: yes—9; no—0

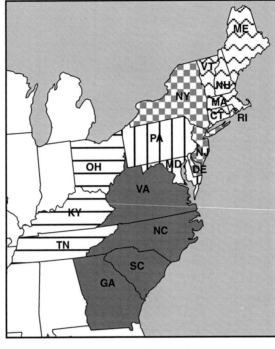

Should the United States Declare War on Britain?

Which regions favored war with England in 1812? _____

Which regions opposed war with England in 1812? _____

How does Document 5 seem to contradict Documents 1, 2, and 4? _____
_____

Document 6

The congressional vote for war, by political party:

Vote Approving the Declaration of War on Britain in 1812 (Both House of Representatives and Senate Votes Combined)			
Federalists		**Democratic-Republicans**	
YES	NO	YES	NO
0	40	98	22

Which party totally opposed the War of 1812? _____

Which party strongly favored the War of 1812? _____

To which party did President Madison belong? _____

(continued)

DBQ 6: The War of 1812 *(continued)*

Document 7

This is an excerpt from a letter written in July 1812 by Congressman Hugh Nelson of Virginia in which he explained why he voted for war. (Quoted from Roger Brown, *The Republic in Peril: 1812,* Columbia University Press, 1964, p. 77)

> . . . to demonstrate to the world . . . that the people of these states were united, one and indivisible . . . to show that our republican government was competent to assert its rights, to maintain the interests of the people, and to repel all foreign aggression . . . My conduct as your representative has been regulated entirely by these great and important considerations.

What reasons did Congressman Nelson give for his support of war in 1812? _____
_____
_____

Document 8
The presidential election of 1812

In November of 1812, President Madison narrowly won reelection against the Federalist candidate DeWitt Clinton, the governor of New York State. The election occurred five months after the war with Britain began.

Which regions of our country supported the reelection of President Madison?

_____

_____

_____

_____

Which regions opposed his reelection?

_____

_____

_____

_____

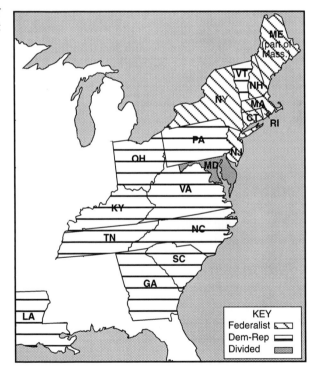

KEY
Federalist
Dem-Rep
Divided

◆ **Part B—Essay**

> *What forces led Americans to declare war on Britain in 1812?*

Grading Key

Document 1

The Congressional Committee reported that Britain was violating our rights to use the ocean and capturing and enslaving our sailors, in spite of repeated protests and complaints.

Document 2

Congressman Calhoun echoes Document 1. America's trading rights are being violated and its citizens harmed by Britain. Calhoun warned that unless Britain stopped these actions, the "honor and interest" of the United States would require us to "resist."

Document 3

Congressman John Randolph was an opponent of war. As this statement shows, he believed that the protection of "maritime rights" was an expedient stratagem and that the real motives of those crying for war were land greed and a desire to annex Canada.

Document 4

In his June 1812 Declaration of War, President Madison pointed to the "lawless violence" of Britain in capturing our ships as the cause of the war.

Document 5

Most congressmen from New England and the maritime middle-Atlantic states were strong opponents of the war. The regions that most favored war were the agricultural Southern, Western, and mid-Atlantic states. This war vote is ironic and seems to contradict earlier documents. If this truly was a war to protect our maritime rights, why didn't the maritime regions support the war?

Document 6

Federalist congressmen unanimously opposed the War of 1812; Democratic-Republican congressmen strongly supported the war. This was a very partisan (political) vote, with President Madison's own party supporting, and the Federalists opposing, the war.

Document 7

Congressman Hugh Nelson told of a number of reasons why he supported the war. In large part he was moved by patriotic motives—to demonstrate that the United States was "one and indivisible," and the superiority of republican government. In part, he was moved by practical motives—to protect American interests and to repel British aggression.

Document 8

The election of 1812, which occurred five months after the war had begun, found the maritime regions of America—New England, New York, and New Jersey—voting for the Federalist candidate. The West and South were united behind Madison and his party. This alignment confirms the pattern seen in Documents 5 and 6. Party politics seemed more important to the war than maritime interests.

Additional Information Beyond the Documents

The documents provide students with only fragments of evidence. Answers should include relevant information from beyond just the documents—information that students have learned from their classroom study. The following list suggests some of the concepts, people, and events that students could use in their essays from their outside learning.

Embargo of 1807	Jefferson	the *Chesapeake* affair
Orders in Council	impressment	Macon's Bill No. 2
Tecumseh	Non-Intercourse Act	old Republicans
Henry Clay	War Hawks	
Hartford Convention	Napoleon	

Unit 4: Jackson, Reform, and Expansion

DBQ 7: Jacksonian Democracy

Historical Context:

A broad-based voting public is essential to any healthy democratic system. American suffrage (the right to vote) has been expanded at different times in our history. In colonial times, suffrage was limited to males, and then typically only to those men who were major landowners and taxpayers. But as years and centuries passed, suffrage was expanded. The most recent episode in this history of democracy's expansion occurred in the early 1970's, when the right to vote was extended to 18-, 19-, and 20-year-olds.

A large increase in the numbers eligible to vote occurred during the 1820's and 1830's. At this time, most states extended suffrage to poor men—factory workers, artisans, laborers, and others who, typically, were not landowners or major taxpayers. This movement to empower the "common man" with the right to vote is sometimes referred to as "Jacksonian democracy." This refers to Andrew Jackson, who championed this cause in his political career, and whose personal life symbolized the rise of the "common man."

The effort to expand suffrage during the "age of Jackson" was a fierce struggle between those who favored it and those who opposed what they saw as a dangerous expansion of democracy. In many ways, the arguments used by supporters and opponents of Jacksonian democracy were similar to those that debated later expansions of voting rights: to African-American men in 1870, to women in 1920, and to 18-, 19-, and 20-year-olds in 1971.

◆ **Directions:** The following question is based on the accompanying documents (1–6). As you analyze the documents, take into account both the source of the document and the author's point of view. Be sure to:

1. Carefully read the document-based question. Consider what you already know about this topic. How would you answer the question if you had no documents to examine?

2. Now, read each document carefully, underlining key phrases and words that address the document-based question. You may also wish to use the margin to make brief notes. Answer the questions which follow each document.

3. Based on your own knowledge and on the information found in the documents, formulate a thesis that directly answers the question.

4. Organize supportive and relevant information into a brief outline.

5. Write a well-organized essay proving your thesis. The essay should be logically presented and should include information both from the documents and from your own knowledge outside of the documents.

> **Question:** *What were the major arguments used, pro and con, in the debate over expanding suffrage during the Age of Jackson? Which arguments were most valid?*

◆ **Part A:** The following documents deal with the debate over Jacksonian democracy. Examine each document carefully, and answer the question or questions that follow.

(continued)

DBQ 7: Jacksonian Democracy *(continued)*

Document 1

In 1821, New York State held a convention to revise the state constitution. A committee recommended dropping the requirement that voters be property owners. This would allow all white male adults the right to vote. The following excerpt shows how Nathan Sanford, the chairman of the committee, supported the recommendation. (From *Reports of the Proceedings and Debates of the Convention of 1821, Assembled for the Purpose of Amending the Constitution of the State of New York*, Albany, New York, 1821.)

> The question before us is the right of suffrage—who shall or who shall not have the right to vote. . . . To me the only qualifications [to vote] seem to be the virtue and morality of the people . . . those who contribute to the public support we consider as entitled to a share of the election of rulers. . . . Now, sir, this scheme will embrace almost the whole male population of the state. . . . This scheme has been proposed by a majority of the committee; they think it safe and beneficial, founded on just and moral principles.

How did Sanford defend the plan to expand the right of suffrage to the poor? _____

_____

_____

Document 2

James Kent, Chief Justice of New York State's highest court, opposed the 1821 proposal to drop property ownership requirements. Here are some of the points he made at the state convention in opposition to Sanford's proposal.

> The tendency of universal suffrage is to jeopardize the rights of property and the principles of liberty. There is a constant . . . tendency in the poor to covet [desire] and to share the plunder of the rich; in the debtor, to relax or avoid the obligation of contracts; in the majority, to tyrannize over the minority and trample down their rights; in the indolent [lazy] and the profligate [depraved] to cast the whole burdens of society upon the industrious and the virtuous; **and there is a tendency in ambitious and wicked men to inflame these combustible materials.**

Why did Kent oppose empowering the poor with the right to vote? _____

_____

_____

What do you suppose Kent meant by "tyrannize over the minority"? _____

_____

_____

What do you suppose he meant by the last line of the quotation? _____

_____

_____

(continued)

Document-Based Assessment
Activities for U.S. History Classes

DBQ 7: Jacksonian Democracy *(continued)*

Document 3

Alexis de Tocqueville, a French nobleman and social observer, visited the United States during the early 1830's. His perceptive observations were collected into a significant book titled *Democracy in America.*

> On my arrival in the United States I was surprised to find so much distinguished talent among the subjects, and so little among the heads of the Government. It is a well-authenticated fact, that at the present day the most able men in the United States are very rarely placed at the head of affairs; and it must be acknowledged that such has been the result in proportion as democracy has outstepped all its former limits. The race of American statesmen has evidently dwindled most remarkably in the course of the last fifty years.
>
> . . . democracy is not only deficient in that soundness of judgment which is necessary to select men really deserving of its confidence, but it has neither the desire nor the inclination to find them . . .

What criticism was Tocqueville making about the expansion of America's democracy? Is his

criticism valid? _____

_____

_____

Document 4

Frances Trollope was an Englishwoman who lived in the United States for several years during the 1820's. She returned to England and in 1832 published *Domestic Manners of the Americans,* a very unflattering account of America, its people, and its culture. The following excerpt from this book describes the election of 1828.

> . . . this electioneering madness . . . engrosses every conversation, it irritates every temper, it substitutes party spirit for personal esteem. When a candidate for any office starts, his party endow him with every virtue, and with all the talents. They are all ready to peck out the eyes of those who oppose him.
>
> When I first arrived in America Mr. John Quincy Adams was President, and it was impossible to doubt, even from the statement of his enemies, that he was every way calculated to do honour to the office. All I ever heard against him was, that "he was too much of a gentleman;" but a new candidate must be set up, and Mr. Adams was out-voted for no other reason, that I could learn, but because it was "best to change." "Jackson for ever!" was, therefore, screamed from the majority of mouths, both drunk and sober, till he was elected.

What, according to Mrs. Trollope, was wrong with America's democracy? _____

_____

_____

(continued)

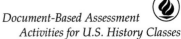

DBQ 7: Jacksonian Democracy *(continued)*

Document 5

George Bancroft was a prominent historian, teacher, and political leader; he served at different times as ambassador to Great Britain, ambassador to Germany, and Secretary of the Navy. The following excerpt comes from a speech he gave at Williams College in 1835.

> . . . the best government rests on the people and not on the few, on persons and not on property, on the free development of public opinion and not on authority . . .
>
> Such is the political system which rests on reason, reflection, and the free expression of deliberate choice. There may be those who scoff at the suggestion that the decision of the whole is to be preferred to the judgment of the enlightened few. They say in their hearts that the masses are ignorant; that farmers know nothing of legislation . . . but true political science does indeed venerate [respect] the masses. . . . Individuals are corrupt [and] false, the masses are ingenuous [open] and sincere. . . .
>
> Thus the opinion which we respect is, indeed, not the opinion of one or of a few, but the sagacity [wisdom] of the many.

What argument did Bancroft make in support of expanding the right to vote to common people?

_____

_____

Document 6

"The County Election" is a painting done by George Caleb Bingham in 1851. The original painting hangs in the St. Louis Art Museum.

Judging by this painting, do you suppose that Bingham was a supporter or an opponent of Jacksonian

Democracy? Support your viewpoint. _____

_____

_____

_____

_____

_____

_____

(continued)

36

DBQ 7: Jacksonian Democracy (continued)

St. Louis Art Museum

◆ **Part B—Essay**

What were the major arguments used, pro and con, in the debate over expanding suffrage during the Age of Jackson? Which arguments were most valid?

Grading Key

Document 1

Sanford supported expanding suffrage to the common man, believing that the "virtue and morality of the people" was a better qualification for voting than wealth and property ownership. Furthermore, even common men contributed to the public support and thus were entitled to the vote.

Document 2

Kent feared giving the vote to common men; it would jeopardize property rights, lead to laws releasing debtors from their debts, and lead to the violation of the rights of minorities by tyrannical majorities. Further, it would encourage wicked politicians to inflame the fears and desires of ignorant voters.

Document 3

Tocqueville believed that the expansion of democracy had actually hurt American politics, discouraging distinguished men from seeking office, and leading the masses to elect less able leaders.

Document 4

Even more than Tocqueville, Mrs. Trollope was repulsed by the coarse and cheap nature of American democratic politics. Party spirit was of more importance than personal esteem, and truly fine statesmen like John Quincy Adams were voted out by the majority, "both drunk and sober." Students may note her snobbish anti-American biases.

Document 5

Bancroft believed that democracy was built on "reason, reflection, and the free expression of deliberate choice," and that political decisions were best made by the "masses" rather than by the "corrupt" and self-serving few.

Document 6

Bingham was a supporter of Jacksonian democracy and celebrated it in his painting. (Several other paintings by Bingham expressed his faith in political democracy. Students may want to see if the school librarian or art teacher can locate reproductions of these paintings.)

Additional Information Beyond the Documents

The documents provide students with only fragments of evidence. Answers should include relevant information from beyond just the documents—information that students have learned from their classroom study. The following list suggests some of the concepts, people, and events that students could use in their essays from their outside learning.

workingmen's parties	Jefferson's views on suffrage	Jackson's bank veto
the spoils system	demands for lenient bankruptcy laws	the Turner thesis
Declaration of Independence	Madison's Federalist Paper #10	industrial social change
Antebellum Reform Era	Democratic and Whig Parties	Nicholas Biddle
the 1829 inauguration	"King Andrew the First"	demagogue
Peggy Eaton affair		

It is significant to note that the question asked in this DBQ has two parts. The second part of the question asks: *Which arguments were most valid?* Good answers will include all kinds of evidence and supportive information, ranging from the Jacksonian era to the present. Grading student answers will require teachers to judge the appropriateness of examples cited, the persuasiveness of the positions argued, and the success with which students presented supportive evidence and data.

Unit 4: Jackson, Reform, and Expansion

DBQ 8: Antebellum Reforms

Historical Context:

No time in America's history has seen greater efforts to reform society than the four decades preceding the Civil War. During those years, a variety of social problems came under attack. Many thousands of Americans worked tirelessly to establish public schooling, reform the criminal justice system, improve care of the infirm and mentally ill, promote women's rights, and battle poverty and drunkenness. By the 1840's and 1850's, abolitionism, the attempt to end slavery, had become the greatest of these antebellum reform movements. (*Antebellum* literally means "before the war." In America's history it marks the decades before the Civil War.) There was, it seemed, an almost frantic effort during the antebellum years to perfect America and its people, to right wrongs and eradicate evils. Mark Hopkins, the president of Williams College, confidently predicted that this huge effort to reform society would soon result in the destruction of "wars, and intemperance, and licentiousness, and fraud, and slavery, and all oppression through the transforming influence of Christianity."

◆ **Directions:** The following question is based on the accompanying documents (1–6). As you analyze the documents, take into account both the source of the document and the author's point of view. Be sure to:

1. Carefully read the document-based question. Consider what you already know about this topic. How would you answer the question if you had no documents to examine?

2. Now, read each document carefully, underlining key phrases and words that address the document-based question. You may also wish to use the margin to make brief notes. Answer the questions which follow each document.

3. Based on your own knowledge and on the information found in the documents, formulate a thesis that directly answers the question.

4. Organize supportive and relevant information into a brief outline.

5. Write a well-organized essay proving your thesis. The essay should be logically presented and should include information both from the documents and from your own knowledge outside of the documents.

Question: *What forces or ideas motivated and inspired this effort to remake and reform American society during the antebellum years?*

◆ **Part A:** Examine each document carefully, and answer the question or questions that follow.

(continued)

DBQ 8: Antebellum Reforms *(continued)*

Document 1

This excerpt is from a statement made by President-elect Andrew Jackson in 1828. (Quoted from *Freedom's Ferment,* by Alice Felt Tyler, Harper & Row, 1961, p. 22.)

> I believe man can be elevated; man can become more and more endowed with divinity; and as he does he becomes more God-like in his character and capable of governing himself. Let us go on elevating our people, perfecting our institutions, until democracy shall reach such a point of perfection that we can acclaim with truth that the voice of the people is the voice of God.

According to this statement by Jackson, what was the ultimate purpose of "elevating our people, [and] perfecting our institutions"? _____

_____

Why was this so important in the 1820's and 1830's?_____

_____

_____

Document 2

William Lloyd Garrison began publishing *The Liberator* in 1831, only two years before founding the American Anti-Slavery Society. Garrison quickly became the most prominent and uncompromising abolitionist in America. The following excerpts come from the first issue of *The Liberator,* in which he publicly vowed to oppose slavery until slavery's "chains are burst . . . SO HELP ME GOD!" He begins by explaining why he decided to establish his abolitionist newspaper in Boston.

> I determined . . . to lift up the standard of emancipation in the eyes of the nation, *within sight of Bunker Hill and in the birthplace of liberty.*
>
> Assenting to the "self evident truth" maintained in the American Declaration of Independence, "that all men are created equal, and endowed by their Creator with certain unalienable rights—among which are life, liberty and the pursuit of happiness," I shall strenuously contend for the immediate enfranchisement [right to vote] of the slave population.

What factors were primary motivations for Garrison in establishing *The Liberator* in Boston?

_____

_____

_____

(continued)

DBQ 8: Antebellum Reforms *(continued)*

Document 3

Francis Grund was a German nobleman who traveled in the United States during the 1830's. Here he describes what he saw as the origin of the antebellum reform spirit.

> Religion has been the basis of the most important American settlements; religion kept their little community together—religion assisted them in their revolutionary struggle; it was religion to which they appealed in defending their liberties. It is with the solemnities of religion that the declaration of independence is yet annually read to the people from the pulpit . . . and it is religion which assists them in all their national undertakings. The Americans look upon religion as a promoter of civil and political liberty.

What, according to Grund, was the inspiration behind Americans' "civil and political" reforms?

_____

_____

_____

Document 4

The most prominent educational reformer of the antebellum years was Horace Mann of Massachusetts. During the years 1837 to 1848 Mann directed the Massachusetts Board of Education; in this role he became a tireless promoter of public education. The following excerpt comes from his Eighth Annual Report to the State Board of Education, issued in 1844.

> If we do not prepare children to become good citizens—if we do not develop their capacities, if we do not enrich their minds with knowledge, imbue their hearts with the love of truth and duty, and a reverence for all things sacred and holy, then our republic must go down to destruction, as others have gone before it.

According to Mann, what was the purpose for public schooling reforms? _____

_____

_____

How does this document compare with Document 1? _____

_____

_____

(continued)

DBQ 8: Antebellum Reforms *(continued)*

Document 5

Theodore Parker, a Massachusetts Unitarian minister, was a leading abolitionist. He was also active in a number of other antebellum reforms, including the peace movement. This is an excerpt from a sermon given in 1847 during America's war with Mexico. (Quoted from *Theodore Parker, Yankee Crusader,* by Henry Steele Commager, The Beacon Press, 1960, p. 192.)

> War is an utter violation of Christianity. . . . If war be right, then Christianity is wrong, false, a lie. Every man who understands Christianity knows that war is wrong.

What, according to this document, inspired Parker's opposition to the Mexican War and his wider involvement in world peace efforts? _____

_____

Document 6

The "Declaration of Sentiments" was issued by the women's rights conventions at Seneca Falls, New York, in July 1848. A number of abolitionists and women's rights advocates, including Elizabeth Cady Stanton, Lucretia Mott, and Frederick Douglass, met in the Wesleyan Chapel in Seneca Falls, a small upstate town. Their goal was to "discuss the social, civil, and religious condition and rights" of American women. Here is an excerpt from the "Declaration of Sentiments," a statement of grievances.

> We hold these truths to be self-evident; that all men and women are created equal; that they are endowed by their Creator with certain inalienable rights; that among these are life, liberty, and the pursuit of happiness; that to secure these rights governments are instituted, deriving their just powers from the consent of the governed. Whenever any form of government becomes destructive of these ends, it is the right of those who suffer from it to refuse allegiance to it, and to insist upon the institution of a new government.

What ideas are suggested here as motives behind the women's rights movement of the antebellum period? _____

_____

◆ **Part B—Essay**

> *What forces or ideas motivated and inspired this effort to remake and reform American society during the antebellum years?*

Grading Key

Document 1

Jackson was expressing a feeling characteristic of this time—that people could improve and perfect themselves. Personal and social improvement was necessary to a self-governing society. (The implication is that as voting rights expanded, it was important that the character and virtue of Americans improve.) That Jackson spoke of man's "God-like" character is significant. This was the time of the Second Great Awakening, and religious motivation for personal and social improvement was strong.

Document 2

Garrison saw slavery as a gross contradiction of America's democratic ideology, a contradiction of the Declaration of Independence, and a violation of the principles of the American Revolution.

Document 3

Grunt pointed out the significance of religion as a motive of "national undertakings" and a "promoter of civil and political liberty." This was an era of religious revival, and, without a doubt, evangelical Protestantism was a major inspiration for this era of reform.

Document 4

As Jackson noted in Document 1, the expansion of democracy during this period motivated efforts to improve the character of the American public. Mann, the foremost promoter of public education during this era, saw schooling as the major way to "imbue" Americans "with the love of truth and duty," virtues necessary to the maintenance of democracy.

Document 5

Parker, like most New England reformers, hated the Mexican War and appealed to Christianity and the teachings of Jesus in order to discredit all wars. Like several other documents, this suggests the importance of the Second Great Awakening as a catalyst of this age of reforms.

Document 6

These early advocates of women's rights appealed to the Declaration of Independence and to democracy in general to support their belief in human equality. (It might be noted that Stanton, Mott, Douglass, and most other participants in this convention were strong abolitionists. Abolitionism itself was a catalyst of the women's rights movement.)

Additional Information Beyond the Documents

The documents provide students with only fragments of evidence. Answers should include relevant information from beyond just the documents—information that students have learned from their classroom study. The following list suggests some of the concepts, people, and events that students could use in their essays from their outside learning.

Charles G. Finney	Second Great Awakening	Jacksonian democracy
temperance	transcendentalism	perfectionism
millennialism	revivals	The Burned Over District
communes	romanticism	the Beecher family
prison reform	Cult of True Womanhood	*Uncle Tom's Cabin*
Robert Owen	Utopian Socialism	nativism

Unit 5: Civil War and Reconstruction

DBQ 9: What Caused Secession?

Historical Context:

No event affected America and its people more significantly than the secession of eleven Southern states and the Civil War that followed. Four years of bloody warfare, over one-half million deaths, untold misery and destruction, and long-lasting racial and sectional hatreds resulted. Even today, almost one and a half centuries later, America is still marked—politically, economically, and socially—by these awful events.

Americans who witnessed the secession of the Southern states, and historians ever since, have argued over the causes. Why, after 85 years of unity and common nationhood, did the United States break apart? Were the differences between North and South so great that unity was no longer possible? Or was secession an accident, the result of mistakes, political misjudgments, and passions that overwhelmed reasonable compromise? What parts did slavery, the debate over its expansion into the territories, and the rancorous conflict of its supporters and opponents play in bringing on secession? How much blame can we place on President Buchanan's indecisiveness? . . . Or on Lincoln's refusal to accept the Crittenden Compromise? And what about the Kansas conflict, Dred Scott, John Brown, and other divisive factors? What were the causes? Who was to blame?

◆ **Directions:** The following question is based on the accompanying documents (1–7). As you analyze the documents, take into account both the source of the document and the author's point of view. Be sure to:

1. Carefully read the document-based question. Consider what you already know about this topic. How would you answer the question if you had no documents to examine?
2. Now, read each document carefully, underlining key phrases and words that address the document-based question. You may also wish to use the margin to make brief notes. Answer the questions which follow each document.
3. Based on your own knowledge and on the information found in the documents, formulate a thesis that directly answers the question.
4. Organize supportive and relevant information into a brief outline.
5. Write a well-organized essay proving your thesis. The essay should be logically presented and should include information both from the documents and from your own knowledge outside of the documents.

> **Question:** *What led the Southern states to secede from the Union in 1860 and 1861?*

◆ **Part A:** The following documents deal with the secession of the Southern states in 1860 and 1861, providing explanations or clues why secession occurred. Examine each document carefully, and answer the question or questions that follow.

Document 1

The following are excerpts from political party platforms during the 1860 presidential campaign. Both platforms were adopted during the summer months.

From the Republican Party platform:

> . . . we deny the authority of Congress, of a territorial legislature, or of any individuals, to give legal existence to slavery in any territory of the United States.

(continued)

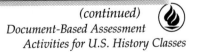

Document-Based Assessment
Activities for U.S. History Classes

DBQ 9: What Caused Secession? *(continued)*

From the (Southern) Democratic Party platform:

> [Speaking of any territory of the United States] . . . all citizens of the United States have an equal right to settle with their property in the Territory, without their rights, either of person or property, being . . . impaired. . . .

Over what issue did the Southern Democratic and the Northern Republican parties seem totally at odds? _____

_____

Do you feel that either side was willing to compromise? _____

_____

Document 2

This excerpt is from a speech given by Albert Gallatin Brown, a Mississippi politician, on September 26, 1860. (From Samuel P. McCutchen, "The Political Career of Albert Gallatin Brown," Doctoral Thesis, University of Chicago, 1930; quoted from Dorothy S. Arnof, *A Sense of the Past*, Macmillan Publishing Company, 1973, p. 222.)

> [The Northerners] hate us now, and they teach their children in their schools and churches to hate our children. . . . The John Brown raid, the burning of Texas, the stealthy tread of abolitionists among us, tell the tale. . . . The North is accumulating power, and it means to use that power to emancipate your slaves. When that is done, no pen can describe . . . the horrors that will overspread this country. . . . Disunion is a fearful thing, but emancipation is worse. Better leave the Union in the open face of day, than be lighted from it at midnight by the [arsonist's] torch.

Why did this Mississippi politician advocate secession? _____

_____

How does this statement help to explain why so many non-slaveholding Southerners supported secession? _____

_____

Document 3

This excerpt is from an editorial in the *Pittsburgh Press*, dated October 10, 1860. This newspaper endorsed Senator Stephen Douglas for president in the 1860 election.

> . . . there is much, if not more, of the rampant spirit of disunion in the Black Republican ranks of the North, as there is in the South. . . . [These Republicans] claim the right to make a code of laws for the South, not only in the States, but in the Territories, which shall control or prohibit slavery. . . . If Lincoln were President . . . the Union would be endangered from that hour.

(continued)

DBQ 9: What Caused Secession? *(continued)*

What do you think of this Pittsburgh newspaper's accusation that Lincoln and his Republican Party are the major threats to the disunion of the country? _____

_____

Document 4

The results of the 1860 presidential election:

Candidate	Popular Vote	Electoral Vote
Lincoln (Republican)	1,865,600	180
Douglas (Democrat)	1,382,700	12
Breckinridge (Democrat)	848,350	72
Bell (Constitutional Union)	592,900	39

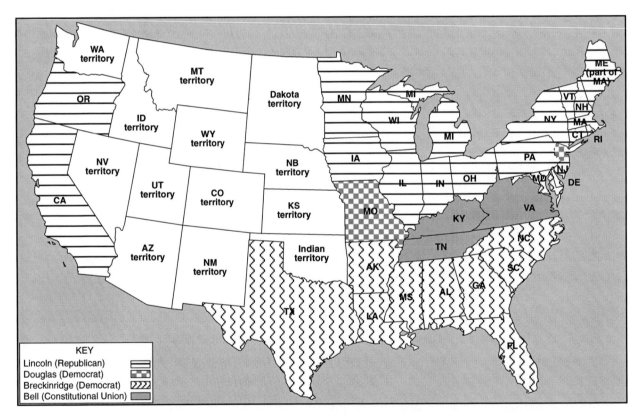

From which region did most of Lincoln's support come? _____

_____

How does Document 2 help to explain this regional voting? _____

_____

(continued)

DBQ 9: What Caused Secession? *(continued)*

Document 5

These excerpts are from the *Diary of George Templeton Strong,* published by The Macmillan Company in 1952. Strong was a prominent New York attorney.

> *November 7, 1860.* Lincoln is elected. Hooray . . . The next ten days will be a critical time. If no Southern state commit itself to treason within a fortnight [two week period] or so, the urgent danger will be past.
>
> *November 10.* . . . . News from the South continues to be menacing and uncomfortable.
>
> *November 12.* No material change in the complexion of Southern news. Unless writers of telegraph items lie loudly, secession is inevitable.
>
> *November 15.* . . . We are generally reconciling ourselves to the prospect of secession by South Carolina, Georgia, Alabama, . . . Florida, and perhaps Mississippi, too.
>
> *November 29.* Thanksgiving Day . . . There's a bad prospect for both sections of the country. Southern ruffianism and brutality are very bad, but the selfishness, baseness, and corruption of the North are no good at all. Universal suffrage . . . [is] at the root of our troubles . . . [the] nucleus [of the crisis] was the abolition handful that . . . till about 1850, was among the more insignificant of our isms. Our feeling at the North till that time was not hostility to slavery, but indifference to it, and reluctance to discuss it. . . . But the clamor of the South about the admission of California ten years ago introduced the question of slavery. . . . That controversy taught us that the two systems could not co-exist in the same territory. It opened our eyes to the fact that there were two hostile elements in the country, and that if we allowed slaves to enter any territorial acquisition, our own free labor must be excluded from it. The question was unfortunate for our peace. But we might have forgotten it had not S. A. Douglas undertaken to get Southern votes by repealing the Missouri Compromise. That was the final blow.

What, according to George Templeton Strong, were the major factors which in the autumn of 1860 were about to split the nation? _____

_____

_____

_____

(continued)

DBQ 9: What Caused Secession? (continued)

Document 6

This excerpt is from the South Carolina ordinance of secession, unanimously approved by the State Legislature on December 20, 1860.

> A geographical line has been drawn across the Union, and all the States north of that line have united in the election of a man to the high office of President of the United States whose opinions and purposes are hostile to Slavery. . . . he has declared that that "Government cannot endure permanently half slave, half free," and that the public mind must rest in the belief that Slavery is in the course of ultimate extinction.

What reason did the state of South Carolina give for seceding from the Union? _____

Document 7

This excerpt is from a letter that Jefferson Davis wrote to George Lunt on January 17, 1861. Davis, a U.S. Senator from Mississippi, was a leader of the Southern states-rights movement. In January 1861 he resigned his seat in the Senate, hoping that he might be chosen commander of the newly formed Confederate army. Instead, he was chosen President of the Confederate States of America, a position he held until the South's defeat in the Civil War. (From *The Papers of Jefferson Davis*, Vol. 7, p. 14. Published by the Louisiana State University Press, 1992.)

> The Election was not the Cause [of secession] it was but the last feather which you know breaks the Camel's back. Sectional hostility manifested in hostile legislation by states and raids of organized bodies sustained by Contributions . . . of northern Society furnish to us sufficient cause. . . .

What did Jefferson Davis say caused the South to secede? _____

What did he mean by "raids of organized bodies"? _____

◆ **Part B—Essay**

> *What led the Southern states to secede from the Union in 1860 and 1861?*

Document-Based Assessment Activities for U.S. History Classes

Grading Key

Document 1

The Southern Democrats and the Northern Republicans held totally opposite beliefs about slavery in the Western territories. The Republicans refused to allow slavery to exist in these territories; the Southern Democrats demanded that slavery be protected wherever it existed.

Document 2

Brown said that the Republicans meant to end slavery and that emancipation would bring ruin and horrors to the South. According to his speech, the Northerners hated the South and were determined to use their growing national power to dominate the South and emancipate its slaves. He advocated that the South secede.

Document 3

This Pittsburgh editor, a supporter of Senator Douglas, argued that Lincoln's election would cause the South to secede because the South could not accept Lincoln's refusal to allow slavery into the Western territories. Note that this is printed only one month before the election.

Document 4

This shows the sectional voting in the presidential election of 1860. Lincoln won only about 40 percent of the popular vote, though a clear majority of the electoral vote. But his support came completely from the North and from the West Coast. Some students may speculate that the Democrats would have won if the party had not split.

Document 5

George Templeton Strong pointed to a number of factors responsible for Southern secession: universal suffrage, abolitionism, the 1850 California statehood crisis (which raised the issue of slavery in the West), and Senator Douglas' repeal of the Missouri Compromise (the Kansas-Nebraska Act). These made obvious the "two hostile elements" that could not coexist in the same country.

Document 6

The South Carolina ordinance of secession stated that the election of Lincoln had united the Northern states against slavery.

Document 7

Jefferson Davis said that the election of Lincoln was only that "last feather" that broke the camel's back. Sectional hostility, the raids of "organized bodies" (suggesting John Brown's raid), and hostile legislation by Northern states were the real causes.

Additional Information Beyond the Documents

The documents provide students with only fragments of evidence. Answers should include relevant information from beyond just the documents—information that students have learned from their classroom study. The following list suggests some of the concepts, people, and events that students could include in their essays from their outside learning.

Fugitive Slave Act	*Uncle Tom's Cabin*	abolition
compromise of 1850	Stephen Douglas	Kansas-Nebraska Act
popular sovereignty	bleeding Kansas	Charles Sumner
Dred Scott decision	Lincoln-Douglas debates	Freeport Doctrine
1860 election	split of the Democratic party	the Tariff Crisis of 1832
Crittendon Compromise		

Name_____ Date_____

Unit 5: Civil War and Reconstruction

DBQ 10: Reconstruction's Failure

Historical Context:

The Civil War may have settled some significant national problems, but it created many more. Yes, slavery was abolished, secession had been refuted, and the supremacy of the national government confirmed. But the cost of Union victory—in lost lives, destroyed property, and sectional bitterness—was staggering, and created huge new problems and tasks.

Perhaps the most challenging task facing our exhausted nation was the future status of the four million newly freed slaves. After the death of President Lincoln and the failure of President Johnson, Congress, in 1867, took charge of the effort to "reconstruct" our divided nation. A large part of "Congressional Reconstruction" was an effort to establish and protect the citizenship rights of the freedmen. The former Confederacy was divided into five military districts, each governed by a Union general. The Southern states, in order to rid themselves of these "military dictatorships," were required to ratify the Fourteenth Amendment, guaranteeing equal rights for all citizens—including the former slaves. At the same time, large numbers of former Confederate soldiers and supporters were disfranchised—denied the right to vote. By 1870 all of the former Confederate states had ratified the Fourteenth Amendment and were readmitted to the union. In each state, the voting rights of freedmen were protected while voting was denied to many white Southerners. And so, with many whites not voting, and union troops remaining in the South to protect them, freedmen seemed to be enjoying some level of equal rights and full citizenship.

But this did not last long; by 1877 Reconstruction had ended. All Southern state governments were restored, and the citizenship rights of the freedmen rapidly eroded. African-American voting rates plummeted. Soon these former slaves fell into a "second class" citizenship characterized by a system of state-enforced segregation and discrimination.

◆ **Directions:** The following question is based on the accompanying documents (1–8). As you analyze the documents, take into account both the source of the document and the author's point of view. Be sure to:

1. Carefully read the document-based question. Consider what you already know about this topic. How would you answer the question if you had no documents to examine?
2. Now, read each document carefully, underlining key phrases and words that address the document-based question. You may also wish to use the margin to make brief notes. Answer the questions which follow each document.
3. Based on your own knowledge and on the information found in the documents, formulate a thesis that directly answers the question.
4. Organize supportive and relevant information into a brief outline.
5. Write a well-organized essay proving your thesis. The essay should be logically presented and should include information both from the documents and from your own knowledge outside of the documents.

> **Question:** *Why did Congress' Reconstruction efforts to ensure equal rights to the freedmen fail?*

◆ **Part A:** The following documents address the reasons why Reconstruction failed in the effort to ensure equal rights to the newly freed slaves. Examine each document carefully, and answer the question or questions that follow.

(continued)

Document-Based Assessment Activities for U.S. History Classes

DBQ 10: Reconstruction's Failure *(continued)*

Document 1

In January 1866, soon after the Thirteenth Amendment ended slavery, radical Republicans in Congress began arguing that freedmen should be allowed to vote on equal terms with whites. A bill was introduced to give the vote to the freedmen of the District of Columbia. Most Democrats and many moderate Republicans opposed this bill, though most radical Republicans supported it (even though only five Northern states allowed African-American men to vote at this time). The following excerpts come from the speech of Pennsylvania Congressman Benjamin Boyer, a Democrat who opposed the bill to enfranchise the African Americans of the District of Columbia.

> It is common for the advocates of negro suffrage to assume that the color of the negro is the main obstacle to his admission to political equality. . . . But it is not the complexion of the negro that degrades him . . . [the Negro is] a race by nature inferior in mental caliber . . . the negroes are not the equals of white Americans, and are not entitled . . . to participate in the Government of this country . . .

Why, according to Congressman Boyer, should African Americans be denied the right to vote?

_____

_____

Do you suppose that this racist viewpoint was widely held at this time? Explain. _____

_____

Document 2

This excerpt, from the report of General George Thomas about activity in Tennessee, was published in the *New York Times* on November 23, 1868.

> With the close of the last, and the beginning of the new year the State of Tennessee was disturbed by the strange operations of a mysterious organization known as the "Kuklux Klan" . . . its grand purpose being to establish a nucleus around which "the adherents of the late rebellion might safely rally."

What, according to General Thomas, was the purpose of the Ku Klux Klan? _____

_____

Look back to the document-based question. How did the Ku Klux Klan help to undermine

Congress' efforts to ensure equal rights to freedmen? _____

_____

_____

(continued)

Document-Based Assessment
Activities for U.S. History Classes

DBQ 10: Reconstruction's Failure *(continued)*

Document 3

This excerpt is from *The Era of Reconstruction, 1865–1877,* by Kenneth M. Stampp (Vintage Books, 1967, p. 193). Stampp was a professor of history at the University of California at Berkeley.

> Meanwhile southern Democrats gained strength when Congress finally removed the political disabilities from most of the prewar leadership. In May 1872, because of pressure from the Liberal Republican, Congress passed a general amnesty act which restored the right of officeholding [and voting] to the vast majority of those who had been disqualified. . . . After the passage of this act only a few hundred ex-Confederates remained unpardoned.

How did the restoration of voting rights to white Southerners undermine efforts to preserve and

protect the voting rights of the freedmen? _____

_____

_____

_____

Document 4

These excerpts are from an editorial in the *Atlanta News,* dated September 10, 1874.

> Let there be White Leagues formed in every town, village and hamlet of the South, and let us organize for the great struggle which seems inevitable.
>
> We have submitted long enough to indignities, and it is time to meet brute-force with brute-force.
>
> If the white democrats of the North are men, they will not stand idly by and see us borne down by northern radicals and half-barbarous negroes. But no matter what they may do, it is time for us to organize.

What is this editorial advocating? _____

_____

_____

_____

_____

(continued)

DBQ 10: Reconstruction's Failure *(continued)*

Document 5

Following are headlines and excerpts from front-page news stories in November 1874.

Headline text from the *New York Times*, November 4, 1874

> *DEMOCRATIC VICTORY*
>
> *CONGRESS TO BE DEMOCRATIC*

Headline and story text from the *New York Times*, November 5, 1874

> *THE REPUBLICAN DEFEAT*
>
> Our later telegrams only add to the magnitude of the defeat experienced on Tuesday. . . . In the House [of Representatives] the Democrats' gains continue to increase in numbers.

How did this Democratic victory help to undermine Congress' efforts to help the freedmen?

_____

_____

What factors discredited the Republican Party during the early 1870's? Explain.

_____

_____

Document 6

In 1935, Dr. W. E. B. DuBois, a prominent African-American historian, published a major history of Reconstruction. Here is a brief excerpt from that book. (From *Black Reconstruction in America*, New York: Atheneum, 1970, p. 693.)

> But the decisive influence was the systematic and overwhelming economic pressure. Negroes who wanted work must not dabble in politics. Negroes who wanted to increase their income must not agitate the Negro problem . . . in order to earn a living, the American Negro was compelled to give up his political power.

According to DuBois, how were freedmen "convinced" to stop voting or taking part in political

events? _____

_____

(continued)

DBQ 10: Reconstruction's Failure *(continued)*

Document 7

During the 1930's, a major effort was made to interview elderly African Americans who could share recollections of their youth in slavery. The following document is an excerpt from an interview with a man named John McCoy. McCoy was born in 1838 and had lived 27 years as a slave in Texas. (Benjamin Botkin, ed., *Lay My Burden Down: A Folk History of Slavery*, University of Chicago Press, 1945, p. 238.)

> Freedom wasn't no different I knows of. I works for Marse John just the same for a long time. He say one morning, "John, you can go out in the field iffen you wants to or you can get out iffen you wants to, 'cause the government say you is free. If you wants to work I'll feed you and give you clothes but can't pay you no money. I ain't got none." Humph, I didn't know nothing what money was, nohow, but I knows I'll git plenty victuals to eat, so I stays . . .

What does this recollection by John McCoy suggest as a reason for the failure of efforts to guarantee freedmen full citizenship rights? _____

_____

Document 8

The disputed presidential election of 1876 set the stage for the final stage of Reconstruction—the removal of all federal troops from the last three "unreconstructed" Southern states: Louisiana, South Carolina, and Florida.

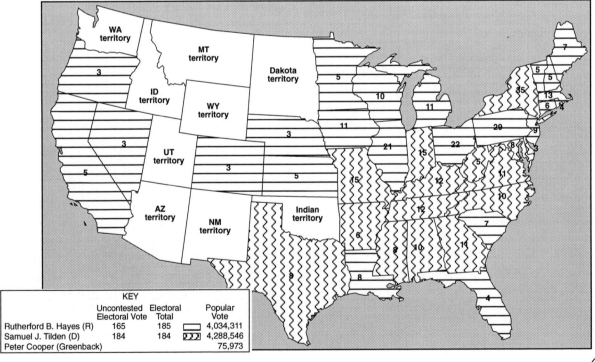

KEY	Uncontested Electoral Vote	Electoral Total		Popular Vote
Rutherford B. Hayes (R)	165	185		4,034,311
Samuel J. Tilden (D)	184	184		4,288,546
Peter Cooper (Greenback)				75,973

DBQ 10: Reconstruction's Failure (continued)

How was it possible that Hayes "won" the election of 1876? _____

_____

_____

_____

_____

How did this disputed election lead to the end of Reconstruction? Explain. _____

_____

_____

_____

_____

◆ **Part B—Essay**

Why did Congress' Reconstruction efforts to ensure equal rights to the freedmen fail?

Grading Key

Document 1

This statement by Boyer, and the fact that only five Northern states allowed African-American men to vote at this time, suggest that white racism was widespread even in the North. One guesses that it was even stronger in the South. Perhaps it was unrealistic to think that racial equality could be achieved at that time.

Document 2

The Ku Klux Klan was organized by white Southerners to undermine radical Reconstruction efforts.

Document 3

Now, with almost all whites allowed to vote again, some Reconstruction state governments were simply voted out of office. White Democratic regimes began to defeat Reconstruction Republican governments, and as the whites "redeemed" their states, freedmen found themselves without protection.

Document 4

The editor of this large Southern newspaper openly called for the formation of "White Leagues" to resist by "brute force" Reconstruction efforts, and called for Northern Democrats to help them overturn the Republican "radicals" and "negroes" who had subjected Southern whites to "indignities."

Document 5

In the 1874 congressional elections the Democrats won control of the House. (Some students may realize that the depression and the Grant scandals had turned many voters against the Republican Party.) Congressional Republicans, severely weakened, began to lose their grip on Reconstruction policy in the South.

Document 6

DuBois suggests that what intimidated and coerced freedmen into abandoning their efforts to vote and maintain equal rights was the fact that freedmen were economically defenseless and vulnerable. Without land and tools, and having few skills, the freedmen were often dependent on whites for their livelihood.

Document 7

This old man, remembering the years after the Civil War, described how indifferent he (and presumably many other freedmen) was about voting and equal citizenship rights. In slavery, they had been kept uneducated and dependent; in freedom, many were unprepared for and disinterested in political involvement.

Document 8

Though historians still don't know all of the details, it is known that deals were made to allow Hayes the presidency in return for his removing Union troops from the last three reconstructed states: Florida, South Carolina, and Louisiana. Reconstruction ended. Efforts by the Northern Republicans in Congress to protect the freedmen and their rights were abandoned.

Additional Information Beyond the Documents

The documents provide students with only fragments of evidence. Answers should include additional relevant information—information that students have learned from their classroom study. The following list suggests some of the concepts, people, and events that students could use in their essays from their outside learning.

Dred Scott decision	radical Reconstruction	Johnson's Plan
Wade-Davis Bill	Freedmen's Bureau	black codes
impeachment	Amendments 13, 14, and 15	Civil Rights Act
Thaddeus Stevens	sharecroppers	Grant scandals
liberal Republicans	radical Reconstruction state	governments
radical Republicans	Tilden-Hayes election	Compromise of 1877
carpetbaggers	scalawags	Force Acts

Unit 6: A Nation in Transition

DBQ 11: The Industrial Boom

Historical Context:

In 1860, the United States was mainly a land of farms and small towns. Fewer than one in five Americans lived in urban areas. (Today the figure is four in five.) While England was rapidly industrializing, the pace of industrial growth was much slower in the United States.

A number of factors seem to have delayed industrialism in the United States. With land plentiful and cheap, and labor relatively scarce and costly, Americans generally found it more profitable to make their livings on farms rather than in factories. And with the western prairies filling up with settlers, it looked in 1860 as if Americans would remain largely a nation of farmers, while England and other European nations became industrial giants.

But only forty years later the United States had become the greatest industrial nation in the world. Between 1860 and 1900, the U.S. production of coal increased from 10,000 short tons to 210,000 short tons, an increase of 2000 percent! Production of steel ingots rose over 5000 percent. By 1900, American workers produced over twice as much steel each year as Germany did, and five times as much as England. Our urban population during these years rose from 6 million to over 30 million. American workers, in huge numbers, were leaving the farms for the factories.

◆ **Directions:** The following question is based on the accompanying documents (1–7). As you analyze the documents, take into account both the source of the document and the author's point of view. Be sure to:

1. Carefully read the document-based question. Consider what you already know about this topic. How would you answer the question if you had no documents to examine?

2. Now, read each document carefully, underlining key phrases and words that address the document-based question. You may also wish to use the margin to make brief notes. Answer the questions which follow each document.

3. Based on your own knowledge and on the information found in the documents, formulate a thesis that directly answers the question.

4. Organize supportive and relevant information into a brief outline.

5. Write a well-organized essay proving your thesis. The essay should be logically presented and should include information both from the documents and from your own knowledge outside of the documents.

> **Question:** *What factors helped to promote America's huge industrial growth during the period from 1860 to 1900?*

◆ **Part A:** The following documents will help you understand the factors that encouraged the development of industry in the last four decades of the nineteenth century. Examine each document carefully, and answer the question or questions that follow.

(continued)

DBQ 11: The Industrial Boom (continued)

Document 1

In the 1850's, the English government sent a committee of businessmen to the United States to study how American industrialists operated their factories. Here is a brief excerpt from the report written in 1854.

> . . . everything that could be done to reduce labour in the movement of materials from one point to another was adopted. This includes mechanical arrangements for lifting material, etc. from one floor to another, carriages for conveying material on the same floor, and such like.

How would the system described above help to cut labor costs and make factory production more efficient? _____

_____

Document 2

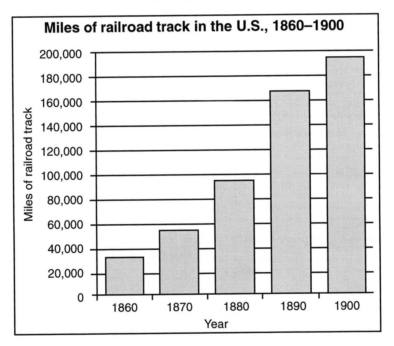

Summarize this information in one short sentence. _____

_____

Explain how the growth of the railroad promoted industrialization. _____

_____

(continued)

DBQ 11: The Industrial Boom (continued)

Document 3

The following are excerpts from the 1860 Republican Party platform.

> . . . sound policy requires . . . an adjustment of . . . imposts [tariffs] . . . to encourage the development of the industrial interests of the whole country. . . .
>
> . . . we commend that policy of national exchanges which secures to the . . . nation commercial prosperity and independence. . . .
>
> . . . the Republican party is opposed to any change in our naturalization laws, or any state legislation by which the rights of . . . immigrants from foreign lands shall be abridged [reduced] or impaired [harmed].
>
> . . . appropriations by Congress for river and harbor improvements . . . required for the accommodation and security of our . . . commerce, are . . . justified by the obligations of government. . . .
>
> . . . a railroad to the Pacific Ocean is imperatively demanded by the interests of the whole country . . . the Federal government ought to render immediate and efficient aid in its construction.

How did these planks (parts) of the Republican platform promote the industrial and

commercial growth of the country? _____

_____

_____

_____

Document 4

Political party control of the presidency, 1860–1900

| Republican | 1861–1865 | 1865–1869 | 1869–1873 | 1873–1877 | 1877–1881 | 1881–1885 | | 1889–1893 | | 1897–1901 |
| Democrat | | | | | | | 1885–1889 | | 1893–1897 | |

1860   1865   1870   1875   1880   1885   1890   1895   1900   1905

How do Documents 3 and 4 help explain why industry boomed in the late nineteenth

century? _____

_____

_____

_____

(continued)

DBQ 11: The Industrial Boom *(continued)*

Document 5

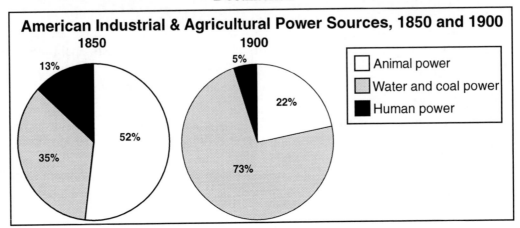

American Industrial & Agricultural Power Sources, 1850 and 1900

1850

13%
52%
35%

1900

5%
22%
73%

☐ Animal power
▨ Water and coal power
■ Human power

How do these charts help to answer the question? _____

_____

Document 6

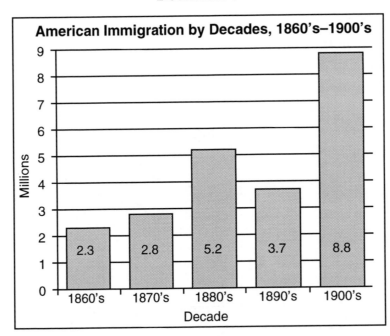

American Immigration by Decades, 1860's–1900's

Millions

Decade	1860's	1870's	1880's	1890's	1900's
	2.3	2.8	5.2	3.7	8.8

Look back to the historical context paragraphs that discuss those factors that slowed the development of industrialism. Document 6 illustrates how one of those factors was overcome. Explain.

_____

_____

(continued)

DBQ 11: The Industrial Boom *(continued)*

Document 7

Andrew Carnegie, one of America's greatest industrialists, was a poor 13-year-old Scottish immigrant when he arrived in Pittsburgh, Pennsylvania, in 1848. By the 1860's, Carnegie was a wealthy and successful businessman. During the years after the Civil War he built Carnegie Steel Company into the largest and most successful steel company in the world. The following document explains, in part, why Carnegie was so successful. (From E. S. Meade, "The Genesis of the United States Steel Corporation," *Quarterly Journal of Economics*, August 1901.)

> In 1882 the Carnegie Steel Company . . . inaugurated a policy whose object was to control all the factors which contributed to the production of steel, from the ore and coal in the ground to the steel billet and the steel rail.

What process was being described here? _____

_____

Which other big industries of the late nineteenth century went through this same process?

_____

_____

_____

◆ **Part B—Essay**

> *What factors helped to promote America's huge industrial growth during the period from 1860 to 1900?*

Grading Key

Document 1

This document describes an early American mill with its conveyer belts and other mechanized systems for moving materials. Americans were the first to effectively use interchangeable parts and assembly line production.

Document 2

Between 1860 and 1900 railroad mileage grew from 30,000 miles to almost 200,000 miles, linking all parts of the nation with a system of rapid and inexpensive transportation and communication. Raw materials, agricultural products, and finished goods could now be easily moved, feeding the growth of industry and commerce.

Document 3

The Republican Party's support of higher tariffs, a national banking system, government aid to build railroads and to improve rivers and harbors, and a liberal immigration policy, all promoted the growth of industry and commerce. This was a "pro-business" platform.

Document 4

Republican Party dominance of the national government during the late nineteenth century helped to encourage pro-business policies, spurring industrial growth.

Document 5

Increasingly, water power, coal, and petroleum were powering America's farms and factories. Certainly these power sources were far superior to animal and human muscle power.

Document 6

A major obstacle to America's industrial growth was the high cost of labor. But with the surge of immigration in the late nineteenth century, this obstacle was largely overcome.

Document 7

Carnegie's steel company was only one of many huge corporate monopolies established in the late nineteenth century. Rockefeller monopolized petroleum production; McCormick monopolized farm machinery; Swift and Armour monopolized meat packing; J. P. Morgan created a banking monopoly; Vanderbilt created a railroad conglomerate; and huge trusts developed in many other parts of the nation's economy.

Additional Information Beyond the Documents

The documents provide students with only fragments of evidence. Answers should include relevant information from beyond just the documents—information that students have learned from their classroom study. The following list suggests some of the concepts, people, and events that students could include in their essays from their outside learning.

factors of production	natural resources	Protestant work ethic
farm mechanization	Civil War spending	public education
Eli Whitney	the Lowell system	textile mills
Anti-Trust Laws	communications	canal system
advantages of incorporation	Social Darwinism	Fourteenth Amendment
labor unionization	imperialism	exploited labor

Unit 6: A Nation in Transition

DBQ 12: The Nativist Response to Immigration

Historical Context:

The Statue of Liberty stands on a small island in New York harbor. This statue is a symbol of America's historic role as a haven for immigrants from all over the world, "yearning to breathe free." In the late nineteenth and early twentieth centuries, the numbers of immigrants seeking a new life in the United States increased greatly. Between 1885 and 1915, almost 20 million immigrants looked up at the Statue as they arrived in America.

In earlier times, immigrants had generally been welcomed. But by the late 1900's, with such huge numbers arriving, many Americans began to grow anxious. Many people began to wonder if the presence of so many foreigners might somehow weaken our society. They worried that it would be impossible to assimilate (absorb) so many immigrants into American society. Few of the new immigrants could speak English. The fact that most of the immigrants were Eastern Orthodox, Catholic, or Jewish at a time when the vast majority of Americans were Protestant, was troubling for many.

People began to speak out against our liberal immigration policies, arguing that we needed laws that would limit immigration. Many people and groups discriminated against immigrants in various ways. And some groups began to openly express their hatred and fear of immigrants. The people who opposed immigration were called "nativists," and their anti-immigrant beliefs were referred to as "nativism."

◆ **Directions:** The following question is based on the accompanying documents (1–7). As you analyze the documents, take into account both the source of the document and the author's point of view. Be sure to:

1. Carefully read the document-based question. Consider what you already know about this topic. How would you answer the question if you had no documents to examine?
2. Now, read each document carefully, underlining key phrases and words that address the document-based question. You may also wish to use the margin to make brief notes. Answer the questions which follow each document.
3. Based on your own knowledge and on the information found in the documents, formulate a thesis that directly answers the question.
4. Organize supportive and relevant information into a brief outline.
5. Write a well-organized essay proving your thesis. The essay should be logically presented and should include information both from the documents and from your own knowledge outside of the documents.

> **Question:** *Why did American nativist groups oppose free, unrestricted immigration in the late nineteenth and early twentieth centuries?*

◆ **Part A:** The following documents are examples of the various nativist statements and arguments for more restrictive immigration laws. Examine each document carefully, and answer the question or questions that follow.

(continued)

DBQ 12: The Nativist Response to Immigration (continued)

Document 1

This excerpt is from a resolution by the American Federation of Labor to Congress, "Some Reasons For Chinese Exclusion, Meat vs. Rice: American Manhood Against Asiatic Coolieism," (1902).

> The Chinese, if permitted freely to enter this country, would create race antagonisms which would ultimately result in great public disturbance. The Caucasians will not tolerate the Mongolian. . . . But this is not alone a race, labor, and political question. It is one which involves our civilization. . . .

What nativist arguments are stated in this document? _____

_____

_____

Consider the source of the statement. What unstated concern do you suspect is the primary

reason why this group opposed Chinese immigration? _____

_____

_____

Document 2

This excerpt is from *Our Country,* by Rev. Josiah Strong (1885).

> . . . immigration not only furnishes the greater portion of our criminals, it is also seriously affecting the morals of the native population. It is disease and not health which is contagious. Most foreigners bring with them continental ideas of the Sabbath, and the result is sadly manifest in all our cities, where it is being transformed from a holy day into a holiday. But by far the most effective instrumentality for debauching [corrupting] popular morals is the liquor traffic, and this is chiefly carried on by foreigners. . . ."

What "diseases" did Strong blame on immigrants? _____

_____

_____

(continued)

Document-Based Assessment Activities for U.S. History Classes

DBQ 12: The Nativist Response to Immigration *(continued)*

Document 3

Many towns, cities, and states sponsored night schools where recent immigrants could learn American customs and how to speak English.

GRANITE CITY

AMERICANIZATION SCHOOLS

Monday
and
Thursday
Evenings
7:30 p. m.

Beginning
Monday,
September
the 27th,
1920

Underwood & Underwood

These two men are brothers, one is an American Citizen and the other has just come to this country with their old mother. See the difference in the way they dress and look. America is a great country. In America everybody has a chance. Everybody who comes to America from the old country ought to learn the American language and become an American citizen. If the people that come to America do not become Americans, this country will soon be like the old country.

SCHOOLS:

HIGH SCHOOL, 20TH AND D STREETS
LINCOLN PLACE, 917 PACIFIC AVENUE

LIBERTY SCHOOL, 20TH AND O STREETS
MADISON SCHOOL, 1322 MADISON AVENUE

Keep America Great.   Become an American Citizen   **Learn The Language.**

Press-Record Publishing Co. 1834 D St., Granite City, Ill

According to this advertisement, why should immigrants learn the "American language"?

_____

_____

_____

_____

_____

(continued)

DBQ 12: The Nativist Response to Immigration *(continued)*

Document 4

Here is an excerpt from a popular book, *The Passing of the Great Race*, by Madison Grant, published in 1916 by Charles Scribner's Sons.

> These new immigrants were no longer exclusively members of the Nordic race as were the earlier ones who came . . . the new immigrants [contain] a large . . . number of the weak, the broken and the mentally crippled of all races drawn from the lowest [levels] of the Mediterranean basin and the Balkans, together with hordes of the wretched, submerged populations of the Polish Ghettos. Our jails, insane asylums and almshouses are filled with this human flotsam [wreckage] and the whole tone of American life, social, moral, and political has been lowered and vulgarized by them.

According to Grant, how were the new immigrants (those who came to America in the late nineteenth and early twentieth centuries) different from earlier immigrant groups?

_____

_____

_____

How did Grant see these newer immigrant groups endangering America? _____

_____

_____

_____

Document 5

During the 1880's and 1890's, many Americans became alarmed over the number of strikes and riots involving labor unions and the many immigrant workers who were union members. This short excerpt comes from "The Age of Steel," a business magazine article that was published soon after the Haymarket Square riot of 1886.

> . . . if the master race of this continent is subordinated to or overrun with the communistic and revolutionary races, it will be in grave danger of social disaster.

According to the author of this article, what was the greatest danger of unrestricted immigration

to the United States? _____

_____

_____

(continued)

DBQ 12: The Nativist Response to Immigration *(continued)*

Document 6

Senator Henry Cabot Lodge of Massachusetts made this statement in 1891. The occasion was a debate in the U.S. Senate over a proposed Literacy Act that would restrict future American immigration to those who could read and write.

> . . . the qualities of the American people . . . are moral far more than intellectual, and it is on the moral qualities of the English-speaking race that our history, our victories, and all our future rest. There is only one way in which you can lower those qualities or weaken those characteristics, and that is by breeding them out. If a lower race mixes with a higher in sufficient numbers, history teaches us that the lower race will prevail. The lower race will absorb the higher. . . .
>
> [We] are exposed to but a single danger, and that is by changing the quality of our race and citizenship through the wholesale infusion of races whose traditions and inheritances, whose thoughts and whose beliefs are wholly alien to ours. . . . There lies the peril at the portals [gates] of our land; there is pressing in the tide of unrestricted immigration. The time has certainly come, if not to stop, at least to check, to sift, and to restrict those immigrants.

What, according to Senator Lodge, was the danger of unrestricted immigration?

_____

_____

Document 7

E. A. Ross was a prominent sociologist early in the twentieth century. This is an excerpt from a magazine article Ross wrote in 1914. (From "Immigrants in Politics," *Century Magazine*, 1914.)

> In every American city with a large, foreign vote have appeared the boss, the machine, and the Tammany way [Tammany Hall was the corrupt city government of New York City]. Once the machine gets a grip on the situation, it broadens and intrenches its power by intimidation at the polls, ballot frauds, vote purchases, saloon influence, and the support of the vicious and criminal. But its tap-root is the simple-minded foreigner . . .

According to Ross, what was the influence of immigrants on American politics and government?

_____

_____

◆ **Part B—Essay**

> *Why did American nativist groups oppose free, unrestricted immigration in the late nineteenth and early twentieth centuries?*

Grading Key

Document 1

The American Federation of Labor wanted to stop the immigration of Chinese workers who, by working for low wages, pulled down the wage rates for all workers. But this statement also reveals the deep racism that was behind this demand.

Document 2

Reverend Strong condemned immigrants for all kinds of sins and threats to American society: corruption, disease, crime, debauching public morals, promoting the liquor trade, and defiling the Sabbath.

Document 3

This advertisement for an "Americanization School" reveals public fears about immigration and the need to quickly try to "Americanize" the foreigners and have them learn the "American" language.

Document 4

This ugly racist statement was widely believed—that immigration was a threat to the purity of the American "Nordic" race and the supremacy of the American civilization.

Document 5

This writer, like many other nativists, blamed the labor and social unrest of the 1880's and 1890's on the radical and dangerous ideas of the "communistic and revolutionary" immigrant "races."

Document 6

Senator Lodge was expressing the fears of many Americans at this time: Unrestricted immigration was corrupting America, its society, its democratic political system, and its moral values. Immigration must be severely restricted.

Document 7

E. A. Ross was expressing a widely-held belief that immigration was subverting America's politics and governmental system.

Additional Information Beyond the Documents

The documents provide students with only fragments of evidence. Answers should include relevant information from beyond just the documents—information that students have learned from their classroom study. The following list suggests some of the concepts, people, and events that students could include in their essays from their outside learning.

Ku Klux Klan	Jim Crow Laws	"new" immigration
labor violence	parochial schools	patterns of assimilation
urban bosses	contributions of immigrants	Social Darwinism
imperialism	anti-Semitism	tenement life
strike breaking	Chinese Exclusion Act	settlement houses
Ellis Island	American Protective Association	Boss Tweed

Unit 7: Populists and Progressives

DBQ 13: The Farmers' Revolt

Historical Context:

Farmers, farming, and country life have always held a special place in the hearts of Americans. Years ago, Thomas Jefferson expressed this when he said

> Those who labor in the earth are the chosen people of God,
> if ever He had a chosen people, whose breasts He
> has made His peculiar deposit for substantial and genuine virtue.

Even today, poets, politicians, artists, movies, and advertisers romanticize the "simple joys and virtues" of country living. During our early history, and well into the nineteenth century, America remained largely a land of farms and small country towns. In many ways, the idealized myth of the "happy and independent farmer" proved true. But in the late nineteenth century farm life for many Americans became harsh and frustrating—far different from the happy myth. Farm income dropped as new farm lands were opened and new machines and methods increased crop yields. Those with smaller farms, poorer lands, or limited resources could no longer compete against the larger and more mechanized farms. Farmers by the thousands went broke and fled to the cities in search of factory jobs.

For the farmers who failed, and for those who struggled and barely succeeded, these were difficult times. Working day after day, from dawn to dusk, and having little or nothing to show for their efforts; watching their wives work and worry themselves to early deaths; seeing their children abandon the farm for the cities—these were the personal agonies shared by thousands across America's agricultural South and West.

The farm crisis came to a head in the 1890's with the organization of the Populist Party. This was a political party, made up mainly of Southern and Western farmers, that hoped to wrench political control of the country from the Democratic and Republican Parties and try to solve the problems that were plaguing rural America. In the presidential election of 1896, the Populists almost succeeded in winning the White House. But, in the end, they failed. Today, fewer than 3 percent of Americans live and work on farms.

◆ **Directions:** The following question is based on the accompanying documents (1–6). As you analyze the documents, take into account both the source of the document and the author's point of view. Be sure to:

1. Carefully read the document-based question. Consider what you already know about this topic. How would you answer the question if you had no documents to examine?

2. Now, read each document carefully, underlining key phrases and words that address the document-based question. You may also wish to use the margin to make brief notes.

3. Based on your own knowledge and on the information found in the documents, formulate a thesis that directly answers the question.

4. Organize supportive and relevant information into a brief outline.

5. Write a well-organized essay proving your thesis. The essay should be logically presented and should include information both from the documents and from your own knowledge outside of the documents.

> **Question:** *What caused the farmers' plight in the late nineteenth century, and how did farmers propose to resolve these problems?*

(continued)

DBQ 13: The Farmers' Revolt (continued)

Document 1

These are excerpts from the 1892 Populist Party platform. In 1892, the Populist Party met in Omaha, Nebraska, where its leaders nominated James Weaver for president. Here are some important statements and demands from the platform.

> We believe that the time has come when the railroad corporations will either own the people or the people must own the railroads.
>
> We demand free and unlimited coinage of silver and gold at the present legal ratio of sixteen to one.
>
> We demand a graduated income tax.
>
> Transportation being a means of exchange and a public necessity, the government should own and operate the railroads in the interest of the people.

Document 2

Washington Gladden was a prominent clergyman in the late nineteenth and early twentieth centuries who believed in applying Christian principles to the social problems of the day. This is an excerpt from an article Gladden wrote in 1890. (From "The Embattled Farmers," published in the *Forum*, November, 1890.)

> The American farmer is steadily losing ground. His burdens are heavier every year and his gains are more meager; he is beginning to fear that he may be sinking into a servile condition. . . . The causes of this lamentable state of things are many . . . protective tariffs, trusts . . . speculation in farm products, over-greedy middlemen, and exorbitant transportation rates. . . . The enormous tribute [payment] which the farmers of the West are paying to the money-lenders of the East, is one source of their poverty. Scarcely a week passes that does not bring to me circulars from banking firms and investment agencies all over the West begging for money to be loaned on farms at eight or nine per cent. . . .

(continued)

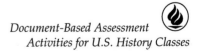

DBQ 13: The Farmers' Revolt (continued)

Document 3

Here is an excerpt from a magazine article, "Causes of Agricultural Unrest," written by James Laurence Laughlin and published in the *Atlantic Monthly* in November of 1896. Laughlin was a professor of economics at the University of Chicago as well as a prominent supporter of the gold standard and opponent of the Populists.

> The simple facts that we produce more wheat than we consume, and that, consequently, the price of the whole crop is determined, not by the markets within this country, but by the world-markets, are sufficient to put wheat, as regards its price, in a different class from those articles whose markets are local.
>
> Feeling the coils of some mysterious power about them, the farmers, in all honesty, have attributed their misfortunes to the "constriction" in prices, caused, as they think, not by an increased production of wheat throughout the world, but by the "scarcity of gold." . . . This explanation of low prices as caused by insufficient gold is so far-fetched that its general use seems inexplicable.

Document 4

The poet Vachel Lindsay was born in Springfield, Illinois in 1879 and raised and educated in the Midwest. This stanza comes from one of his poems entitled "BRYAN, BRYAN, BRYAN, BRYAN: The Campaign of Eighteen Ninety-six, as Viewed at the Time by a Sixteen Year Old, etc."

> Election night at midnight:
> Boy Bryan's defeat.
> Defeat of western silver.
> Defeat of the wheat.
> Victory of letterfiles
> And plutocrats in miles
> With dollar signs upon their coats,
> Diamond watchchains on their vests
> And spats on their feet.
> Victory of custodians.
> Plymouth Rock,
> And all that inbred landlord stock.
> Victory of the neat.
> Defeat of the aspen groves of Colorado valleys,
> The blue bells of the Rockies,
> And blue bonnets of old Texas,
> By the Pittsburgh alleys.
> Defeat of alfalfa and the Mariposa lily.
> Defeat of the Pacific and the long Mississippi.
> Defeat of the young by the old and silly.
> Defeat of tornadoes by the poison vats supreme.
> Defeat of my boyhood, defeat of my dream.

(continued)

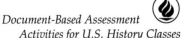

DBQ 13: The Farmers' Revolt *(continued)*

Document 5

Production and Prices, 1860–1895

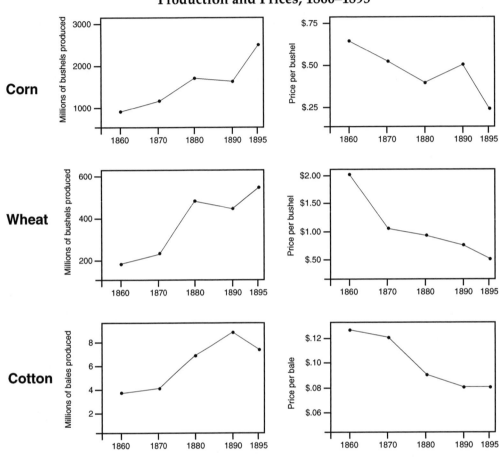

Corn

Wheat

Cotton

Document 6

Here is an excerpt from a letter written by a farmer to the editor of a Populist newspaper in Lincoln, Nebraska. (F. Houchin to the editor of *Wealth Makers*, May 1, 1895. Quoted in *The Populist Response to Industrial America*, by Norman Pollack, Harvard University Press, 1962, p. 112.)

> We will get permanent relief only when the government owns the railroads and when we have government banks where we can get money at a small rate of interest.

Question: *What caused the farmers' plight in the late nineteenth century, and how did farmers propose to resolve these problems?*

Grading Key

Document 1

The Populists wanted the protection from exorbitant railroad rates that government ownership would provide. They also sought a graduated income tax, one that would tax the wealthy at a higher rate. And, believing that monetary inflation would raise farm prices, they sought "free silver."

Document 2

According to Washington Gladden, the farmers' plight grew from a high protective tariff that made manufactured goods expensive, the existence of business trusts that could exploit consumers, greedy middlemen, exorbitant railroad rates, and bank interest rates.

Document 3

Laughlin believed that the farmers' problems were a result of overproduction of farm produce and the fact that, because American farmers were now a part of a world market, production changes anywhere in the world would have a large impact on the prices American farmers received for their crops. The farmers' complaint about a "scarcity of gold" was simply incorrect. The fact that "we produce more wheat than we consume" drove prices down.

Document 4

The beauty of this stanza is its contrast of the victors—"plutocrats . . . with dollar signs upon their coats," "the landlord stock," and "the neat" with those who went down to defeat with Bryan, the "defeat of western silver, defeat of the wheat . . . defeat of my boyhood, defeat of my dream." Obviously this romanticized verse is hardly objective, but it does explain how many farmers saw the 1896 election results.

Document 5

These graphs suggest that Laughlin (Document 3) was right; higher production led to lower prices. Thus, individual farmers were in a quandary; the harder they worked, the more they grew, and the less they earned. This frustration helps explain both the farmers' anger and why they seemed so open to "conspiracy theories" about the causes of their crisis.

Document 6

This letter simply reiterates earlier documents. Many Populists felt that the only way to escape the exorbitant rail rates and bank interest rates was to have the government own the banks and railroads and operate them in the public interest.

Unit 7: Populists and Progressives

DBQ 14: Progressivism

Historical Context:

For almost a century historians have argued about progressivism: What were its defining characteristics? What was its meaning? What did progressivism accomplish? They can agree on some points: Yes, the progressive era was generally a period of social, political, and economic reforms; and yes, it lasted for only a few years, from about 1900 to 1917 (though some historians say it began earlier and some say it lasted longer). As to its characteristics, most historians would say that progressives were generally optimists, believing that social ills were curable. Most progressives were middle class and educated. Most were Protestant, and the sense of religious fervor and mission ran through their rhetoric and their work. Much (but certainly not all) of the progressives' focus was on urban America and its problems. And, progressivism's tone was distinctly moral, idealistic, and patriotic. But beyond these few general points, there is little agreement. Perhaps the only thing that *all* historians would agree upon is this: Progressivism is not easily understood, and it was certainly broader, more varied, and more complicated than it's often described in high school history books.

◆ **Directions:** The following question is based on the accompanying documents (1–9). As you analyze the documents, take into account both the source of the document and the author's point of view. Be sure to:

1. Carefully read the document-based question. Consider what you already know about this topic. How would you answer the question if you had no documents to examine?

2. Now, read each document carefully, underlining key phrases and words that address the document-based question. You may also wish to use the margin to make brief notes.

3. Based upon your own knowledge of the topic and on the evidence found in the documents, formulate a thesis that directly answers the question.

4. Organize supportive and relevant information into a brief outline.

5. Write a well-organized essay proving your thesis. The essay should be logically presented and should include information both from the documents and from your own knowledge outside of the documents.

Question: *How would you define and describe the progressive reform movement?*

(continued)

DBQ 14: Progressivism (continued)

Document 1

Here is a brief excerpt from a speech given by U.S. Senator Elihu Root in 1913. Root had earlier served in President Theodore Roosevelt's cabinet as Secretary of War and Secretary of State. In 1912 he was awarded the Nobel Peace Prize. In this section of his speech, Root is explaining why the progressive reform movement began. (Be warned: This is a difficult reading and will take some effort to understand.)

> The real difficulty appears to be that the new conditions [growing from] the . . . industrial development of the last half-century are continuously and progressively demanding the readjustment of the relations between [society] and the establishment of new legal rights and obligations not [understood or anticipated in America's early years] when . . . laws were passed or . . . limitations upon the powers of government were [placed] in our Constitution.

Document 2

This short excerpt comes from the first inaugural address of President Woodrow Wilson, given on March 4, 1913. Early in the speech, Wilson reminded Americans that industrialism had brought us great material wealth.

> We see that in many things [our] life is very great. . . . But . . . evil has come with the good. . . . With riches has come inexcusable waste. We have squandered a great part of what we might have used, and have not stopped to conserve the exceeding bounty of nature. . . . We have been proud of our industrial achievements, but we have not . . . stopped thoughtfully enough to count the human costs. . . . [Our] great Government we loved has too often been made use of for private and selfish purposes, and those who used it had forgotten the people.
>
> At last a vision has been [shown to] us of our life as a whole. We see the bad with the good. . . . With this vision we approach new affairs. Our duty is to cleanse, to reconsider, to restore, to correct the evil . . . to purify and humanize every process of our common life. . . .

(continued)

DBQ 14: Progressivism *(continued)*

Document 3

In 1912, four years after retiring from the presidency, Theodore Roosevelt again ran for president. He ran, not as the Republican Party candidate, but as the candidate of a third party, the Progressive Party. This document is a short excerpt from the keynote address given by U.S. Senator Albert Beveridge at the 1912 Progressive Party convention in Chicago.

> We stand for a nobler America. We stand for an undivided Nation. We stand for a broader liberty, a fuller justice. We stand for social brotherhood as against savage individualism. We stand for an intelligent cooperation instead of a reckless competition. We stand for mutual helpfulness instead of mutual hatred. We stand for equal rights, as a fact of life instead of a catchword of politics. We stand for the rule of the people as a practical truth instead of a meaningless pretense. We stand for a representative government that represents the people. We battle for the actual rights of man.

Document 4

John Spargo was a progressive muckraker and, like many other muckrakers, an active socialist. He focused much of his reform efforts on improving the lives of poor children. The following quotation comes from the introduction to a book he wrote in 1908; in it, he advocated government controls over the pasteurization and sale of milk in order to protect the health of babies and children. (From John Spargo, *The Common Sense of the Milk Question*, Macmillan, 1908.)

> What I want to do is to place before the American public a calm and dispassionate statement of certain curable ills as a basis upon which to rest an earnest plea for action; to waken, if possible, all those dormant and neglected powers and impulses for good which need to be called into active cooperation in order that the evils may be remedied.

Document 5

Here is another brief quote from John Spargo. This comes from a letter that he wrote to historian Louis Filler in 1938, in which he tried to explain the goals of socialist muckrakers like himself, Upton Sinclair, Robert Hunter, Rhetta Child Dorr, Lincoln Steffens, and many others during the progressive era, years earlier.

> The things we were advocating were not advocated with a view to overturning the capitalist system. All that we wrote might as well have been written by an earnest Christian trying to apply Christian principles to a very definite and serious human problem.

(continued)

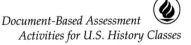

DBQ 14: Progressivism (continued)

Document 6

Here is an excerpt from a speech given by President Theodore Roosevelt to the National Conservation Congress in 1908.

> . . . there must be the look ahead, there must be a realization of the fact that to waste, to destroy, our natural resources, to skin and exhaust the land instead of using it so as to increase its usefulness, will result in undermining in the days of our children the very prosperity which we ought by right to hand down to them amplified and developed.

Document 7

This is a brief excerpt from *The Struggle for Self-Government*, a book written by Lincoln Steffens and published in 1906.

> Too often we have found both [political] parties representing graft—big business graft. The people, especially in the West, are waking to a realization of this state of things, and . . . they are following leaders who see that the way to restore government representative of the common interests of the city or State is to restore to public opinion the control of the dominant party. . . . The people of Wisconsin . . . are law-abiding, conservative, and fair. . . . And they are to be trusted, for no matter how men may differ about Governor La Follette otherwise, his long, hard fight has developed citizenship in Wisconsin—honest, reasonable, intelligent citizenship.

Document 8

This is a list of some of the significant areas of reform during the progressive era.

Women's suffrage	Child labor laws	Anti-Trust laws
Food and drug inspection	Local building codes	Local fire codes
Milk pasteurization laws	Prohibition	Antiprostitution laws
Settlement houses	Social Gospel	Professional licensing
Progressive income taxes	Election reforms	Referendum and Initiative
Election of U.S. Senators	Conservation laws	National and State parks
Clean government reforms	Labor laws	School attendance laws
Federal Reserve Act	Interstate commerce	Civil Service reforms
Worker safety laws	Tariff reforms	Progressive education
World peace movements		

(continued)

Document-Based Assessment
Activities for U.S. History Classes

DBQ 14: Progressivism *(continued)*

Document 9

Here is an excerpt from the "Social Creed of the Methodist Episcopal Church," a statement adopted in 1908.

The Methodist Episcopal Church stands:

For equal rights and complete justice for all men in all stations of life.

For the abolition of child labor.

For such regulation of the conditions of labor for women as shall safeguard the physical and moral health of the community.

For a release from employment one day in seven.

For a living wage in every industry.

For the highest wage that each industry can afford and for the most equitable division of the products of industry that can ultimately be devised.

For the recognition of the Golden Rule and the mind of Christ as the supreme law of society and the sure remedy for all social ills.

Grading Key

Document 1

Senator Root believed that the progressive reform movement was an attempt to readjust society, its laws and social relations, to address the needs created by industrial and urban development.

Document 2

President Wilson, in his Inaugural Address, said much the same thing stated in Document 1. Modern industrialism brought America greatness and riches, but also evil, waste, human costs, and government corruption. It was, Wilson believed, the duty of progressives to "cleanse, to reconsider, to restore, to correct the evil . . . to purify and humanize every process of our common life. . . ."

Document 3

Senator Beveridge stated a number of key characteristics of progressivism—social justice, equal rights, a clean government responsive to the "people," and humane controls on "savage individualism" and business.

Document 4

Spargo described the general belief of the muckrakers—that exposing social ills to the American public would awaken "impulses for good" that would be united into demands that these "evils may be remedied."

Document 5

Many muckrakers and progressive leaders were socialists, but most were motivated as much (or more) by Christian principles as by Marxism.

Document 6

Conservation was a major part of the progressive reform effort. As with other parts of progressivism, it grew from needs created by unrestrained and unplanned industrial growth.

Document 7

Government reform at the local, state, and national levels was central to the progressive movement. In this document, muckraker Lincoln Steffens (best known as author of *The Shame of the Cities*) praised the people of Wisconsin for supporting Governor Robert La Follette who was a champion of clean government.

Document 8

This list shows that progressivism was broadly defined, including comprehensive efforts aimed at reforming all aspects of American life. It was not just a movement for government reform.

Document 9

As this document shows, churches and organized religion were active in the reform efforts of the progressive era—attempting to apply the Golden Rule and the teachings of Jesus Christ to modern life.

Additional Information Beyond the Documents

The documents provide students with only fragments of evidence. Answers should include relevant information from beyond just the documents—information that students have learned from their classroom study. The following list suggests some of the concepts, people, and events that students could include in their essays from their outside learning. (Note that Document 8 lists many of the various components of progressivism.)

Jane Addams and Hull House	Upton Sinclair's *The Jungle*	TR's Trust busting
Niagara movement and NAACP	Jacob Riis	New Nationalism
new freedom	Federal Reserve System	Hepburn Act
Northern securities case	social control	new immigrants
bossism	Gifford Pinchot	J. P. Morgan
Eugene Debs	Christian socialism	social gospel

Unit 8: World Expansion and New Responsibilities

DBQ 15: The Debate Over American Imperialism

Historical Context:

The closing decades of the nineteenth century saw a great scramble for empire as England, France, Germany, and other major industrial nations took control of areas of Africa, the Middle East, Asia, and other regions of the world. What prompted the rise of imperialism? Sometimes colonies provided industrial nations with raw materials for their factories or captive markets for their manufactured goods. Sometimes colonies were sought for military or strategic purposes, providing coaling stations for coal-fired, steam-driven naval vessels or offering geographic locations of critical importance. Sometimes colonies were obtained for national prestige. Many people at this time felt that great nations proved their greatness by conquering and controlling large empires. Countries bragged about their empires. Boasting of their immense empire, which literally spanned the entire world, the British gloated that "the sun never sets on Great Britain."

During most of the nineteenth century, the United States ignored this scramble for overseas empires. Americans were busy conquering their own continent, spreading settlements across the broad prairies, the Great Plains, over the Rockies to the Pacific coast. An overseas empire attracted little interest until the very end of the nineteenth century. Then, in a matter of months, overseas colonies and the allure of national empire captured the interest of the American public.

America's new interest in colonial empire grew largely from the 1898 Spanish-American War. Begun to help Cuba free itself from Spanish colonial rule, the war was, for Americans, something of a lark, quickly won with few casualties. But there was great irony in our victory. Begun to champion the cause of anti-colonialism, the war ended with the United States in possession of its own colonial empire. Should we annex Puerto Rico, Guam, and the Philippines, former Spanish colonies which now were ours? From the war's end in August 1898 until the U.S. Senate ratified the Treaty of Paris in February 1899 annexing these regions, a nationwide debate raged: Should the United States, a nation born in a revolt against colonialism, now become a colonial nation itself? Should we, a people who profess to believe in democracy and self-rule, now become the imperial rulers of colonial peoples? And even after the debate was supposedly settled with the February 1899 Senate vote, heated discussion continued. This national argument over imperialism became even more passionate after the Filipinos took up arms against American occupation, beginning two years of bloody jungle fighting with U.S. troops. And, as national debates often do, this domestic quarrel over imperialism became a major political issue, greatly influencing the presidential election of 1900.

◆ **Directions:** The following question is based on the accompanying documents (1–7). As you analyze the documents, take into account both the source of each document and the author's point of view. Be sure to:

1. Carefully read the document-based question. Consider what you already know about this topic. How would you answer the question if you had no documents to examine?

2. Now, read each document carefully, underlining key phrases and words that address the document-based question. You may also wish to use the margin to make brief notes.

3. Based upon your own knowledge of the topic and on the evidence found in the documents, formulate a thesis that directly answers the question.

(continued)

DBQ 15: The Debate Over American Imperialism *(continued)*

4. Organize supportive and relevant information into a brief outline.
5. Write a well-organized essay proving your thesis. The essay should be logically presented and should include information both from the documents and from your knowledge outside of the documents.

> **Question:** *Was imperialism a proper and legitimate policy for the United States to follow at the turn of the nineteenth century?*

Document 1

More than a decade before the Spanish-American War, Rev. Josiah Strong, a prominent Protestant clergyman, wrote *Our Country,* a book that became both popular and influential. This passage, taken from Strong's book, advocates imperialism as a policy of the United States.

> It seems to me that God, with infinite wisdom and skill, is training the Anglo-Saxon race [Strong meant Americans of British and German descent] for an hour sure to come in the world's future. . . . this race of unequaled energy, with all the majesty of numbers and the might of wealth behind it—the representatives . . . of the largest liberty, the purest Christianity, the highest civilization . . . will spread itself over the earth. . . . this powerful race will move down upon Mexico, down upon Central and South America, out upon the islands of the sea, over upon Africa and beyond. And can any one doubt that the result of this competition of races will be the "survival of the fittest?"

Document 2

Another American proponent of imperialism was a top U.S. Navy officer, Alfred T. Mahan. Mahan's views were well known and popular with many. This excerpt comes from a book he wrote shortly before the Spanish-American War, titled *The Interest of America in Sea Power* (1897).

> Americans must begin to look outward. The growing production of the country demands it. An increasing volume of public sentiment demands it. The position of the United States, between the two Old Worlds and the two great oceans, makes the same claim.

(continued)

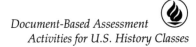

*Document-Based Assessment
Activities for U.S. History Classes*

DBQ 15: The Debate Over American Imperialism *(continued)*

Document 3

The initial decision whether or not to annex the Philippines was made by President McKinley. In the following excerpt, he explains why he recommended annexation to the U.S. Senate. He was speaking to a group of religious leaders when he made this statement.

> I walked the floor of the White House night after night until midnight; and I am not ashamed to tell you, gentlemen, that I went down on my knees and prayed Almighty God for light and guidance. . . . And one night late it came to me this way . . .
>
> 1. That we could not give them back to Spain—that would be cowardly and dishonorable;
>
> 2. that we could not turn them over to France or Germany—our commercial rivals in the Orient—that would be bad business and discreditable;
>
> 3. that we could not leave them to themselves—they were unfit for self-government—and they would soon have anarchy and misrule there worse than Spain's was; and
>
> 4. that there was nothing left for us to do but to take them all, and to educate the Filipinos, and uplift and civilize and Christianize them, and by God's grace do the very best we could by them, as our fellowmen for whom Christ also died.

Document 4

U.S. Senator George F. Hoar represented Massachusetts in Congress from 1869 until his death in 1904, and was a major opponent of imperialism. The following excerpt comes from a speech Hoar made in January 1899, in opposition to the treaty annexing the Philippines.

> . . . the question with which we now have to deal is whether Congress may conquer and may govern, without their consent and against their will, a foreign nation, a separate, distinct, and numerous people, a territory not hereafter to be populated by Americans. . . .
>
> . . . under the Declaration of Independence you cannot govern a foreign territory, a foreign people, another people than your own . . . you cannot subjugate them and govern them against their will, because you think it is for their good, when they do not; because you think you are going to give them the blessings of liberty. You have no right at the cannon's mouth to impose on an unwilling people your Declaration of Independence and your Constitution and your notions of freedom and notions of what is good.

(continued)

DBQ 15: The Debate Over American Imperialism *(continued)*

Document 5

Albert Beveridge, a Republican senator from Indiana, supported imperialism. How did he justify this policy in the following excerpt from a speech he made in the U.S. Senate in 1900?

> The Philippines are ours forever. . . . We will not retreat. . . . We will not repudiate [renounce] our duty. . . . We will not abandon our opportunity in the Orient. We will not renounce our part in the mission of our race, trustee, under God, of the civilization of the world. And we will move forward to our work . . . with gratitude . . . to Almighty God that He has marked us as His chosen people, henceforth to lead in the regeneration of the world. . . .
>
> . . . the Pacific is the ocean of the commerce of the future. . . . The power that rules the Pacific . . . is the power that rules the world.

Document 6

Henry Cabot Lodge, a Republican senator from Massachusetts, also supported imperialism. How did Lodge defend imperialism in this statement from a Senate speech made in 1900?

> . . . we are in the Philippines as righteously [honorably] as we are there rightly and legally.
>
> . . . The taking of the Philippines does not violate the principles of the Declaration of Independence, but will spread them among a people who have never known liberty, and who in a few years will be as unwilling to leave the shelter of the American flag as those of any other territory we ever brought beneath its folds.

Document 7

The prospect of the United States becoming an imperialistic nation galvanized a strong opposition, and many opponents rallied around the newly created American Anti-Imperialist League. Here are some excerpts from the Anti-Imperialist League's platform which was adopted during the 1900 presidential campaign.

> We hold that the policy known as imperialism is hostile to liberty and tends toward militarism, an evil from which it has been our glory to be free. We regret that it has become necessary in the land of Washington and Lincoln to reaffirm that all men, of whatever race or color, are entitled to life, liberty and the pursuit of happiness. We maintain that governments derive their just powers from the consent of the governed. We insist that the subjugation of any people is "criminal aggression."
>
> . . . We hold, with Abraham Lincoln, that "no man is good enough to govern another man without that other's consent."

Grading Key

Document 1

The late nineteenth century was a time when racism, as expressed in Social Darwinism, was widely believed. In this selection from *Our Country*, this racist tone is obvious. Strong believed that American Anglo-Saxons were destined to rule the world, spreading their political and religious tenets to all others. This, he believed, was part of nature's and God's design.

Document 2

Alfred Mahan was urging Americans to "look outward," to take our own colonial empire. The demands of modern trade, our geographic position in the world, and public sentiment "demanded" this.

Document 3

President McKinley was expressing what many Americans felt. This was a time of arrogant nationalism, when many Americans truly did feel that "lesser peoples" would benefit from American rule. It was, he felt, our duty. He suggested another reason—that if we did not take the Philippines, someone else (France? Germany?) would. Many Americans found this a persuasive argument. (Students may want to look more closely at McKinley's desire to "Christianize" the Filipino people. What religion were most Filipinos at this time?)

Document 4

Senator Hoar felt that imperial control of other peoples was a gross violation of the democratic principles upon which America was established. And, as this statement shows, he did not share the ethnocentric and arrogant nationalism that McKinley expressed in Document 3.

Document 5

Senator Beveridge's nationalistic rhetoric was widely applauded. It was, he felt, our duty to God, to posterity, to civilization, to the "mission of our race" to annex the Philippines and to bring it the benefit of our rule. As Mahan did, Beveridge also noted the commercial and strategic benefits that colonial empire would bring.

Document 6

Senator Lodge was another strong supporter of imperial empire. Here he tried to refute the argument that Senator Hoar used in Document 4. Annexation of the Philippines, he argued, was not a violation of the Declaration of Independence, but an expansion of these democratic principles.

Document 7

The Anti-Imperialist League tried to discredit imperialism by pointing to its violation of democratic principles and by associating those principles with Washington and Lincoln. Note also how the prose borrows directly from the Declaration of Independence.

Additional Information Beyond the Documents

The documents provide students with only fragments of evidence. Answers should include relevant information from beyond just the documents—information that students have learned from their classroom study. The following list suggests some of the concepts, people, and events that students could include in their essays from their outside learning.

Hawaii	Social Darwinism	Theodore Roosevelt
Monroe Doctrine	Venezuelan crises	Platt Amendment
Teller Amendment	Aguinaldo	the *Maine*
yellow press	Open Door Policy	William Jennings Bryan
Panama	Dollar Diplomacy	the Turner thesis

Unit 8: World Expansion and New Responsibilities

DBQ 16: Why Did We Enter World War I?

Historical Context:

When the Great War broke out in the summer of 1914, Americans were shocked at the barbarism of modern warfare. They were thankful for the Atlantic Ocean which separated our country from the warring nations of Europe. People were determined to keep out of the conflict and applauded President Wilson when he asked that his fellow citizens remain "neutral in fact as well as in name."

Through the following months, while national resolve to remain neutral stayed strong, many Americans began to choose sides. This was almost inevitable. Most Americans could trace family roots to England, Germany, Italy, Eastern Europe, or other countries or regions then engulfed by war. In fact, many were themselves immigrants or the children of immigrants from one of the nations at war. It was only natural that they still had emotional ties to their homelands. Many people, shocked and appalled by Germany's brutal invasion of Belgium in the opening weeks of the war, were firm opponents of the Germans. Many others aligned their sympathies with France, remembering that the French had aided us in our war of independence. As American shipping and trade began to be blocked by England and Germany, patriotic anger rose. But still, even after German submarines sank the British liner *Lusitania* in May of 1915, killing over 100 Americans, public opinion still opposed American involvement in the war. In November 1916, American determination to stay out of the war expressed itself in reelecting President Wilson whose campaign slogan was "He kept us out of War."

Nonetheless, April 2, 1917 found President Wilson standing before a joint session of Congress asking that war be declared against Germany. "I advise that the Congress declare the recent course of the Imperial German government to be, in fact, nothing less than war against the government and people of the United States." Two days later the Senate voted 82 to 6 for war. Then, on April 6, the House of Representatives did the same, voting 373 to 50.

What led the United States to abandon its neutrality and isolation? What led Americans into World War I?

◆ **Directions:** The following question is based on the accompanying documents (1–7). As you analyze the documents, take into account both the source of each document and the author's point of view. Be sure to:

1. Carefully read the document-based question. Consider what you already know about this topic. How would you answer the question if you had no documents to examine?

2. Now, read each document carefully, underlining key phrases and words that address the document-based question. You may also wish to use the margin to make brief notes.

3. Based upon your own knowledge of the topic and on the evidence found in the documents, formulate a thesis that directly answers the question.

4. Organize supportive and relevant information into a brief outline.

5. Write a well-organized essay proving your thesis. The essay should be logically presented and should include information both from the documents and from your knowledge outside of the documents.

> **Question:** *Why did the United States abandon its neutrality, choosing to enter World War I on the side of the allies?*

(continued)

DBQ 16: Why Did We Enter World War I? *(continued)*

Document 1

When the war broke out in Europe, William Jennings Bryan was serving as President Wilson's Secretary of State. On August 10, 1914 (only two weeks after the outbreak of the war), Secretary Bryan sent President Wilson the following message.

> Morgan Company of New York [a large Wall Street investment bank] have asked whether there would be any objection to their making a loan to the French Government. . . . [I would question] whether it would be advisable for this Government to . . . approve . . . any loan to a belligerent nation. . . . Money is the worst of all contraband because it commands every-thing else. . . . I know of nothing that would do more to prevent war than an international agreement that neutral nations would not loan to belligerents. . . . The powerful financial interests which would be connected with these loans would be tempted to use their influence through the newspapers to support the interests of the Government to which they had loaned because the value of the [loan] would be directly affected by the result of the war. . . . All of this influence would make it all the more difficult for us to maintain neutrality [with] powerful financial interests . . . thrown into the balance. . . .

Document 2

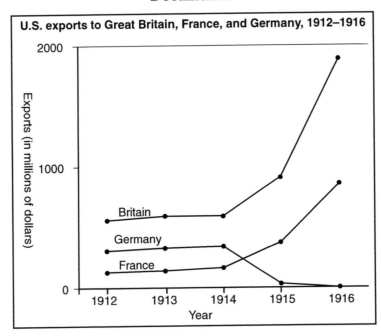

U.S. exports to Great Britain, France, and Germany, 1912–1916

(continued)

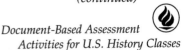

DBQ 16: Why Did We Enter World War I? *(continued)*

Document 3

Our entrance into the war in 1917 found us allied with England, France, and Russia. But the year 1917 also saw revolutionary upheaval in Russia. In the autumn, the Bolsheviks (communists), under the leadership of Lenin, took control of the country. Within months Russia dropped out of the war. In August of 1918, Lenin released a letter to American workers. These excerpts come from that letter.

> The results of the four years of war have revealed the general law of capitalism as applied to war between robbers for the division of spoils; the richest and strongest profited and grabbed most, while the weakest were utterly robbed, tormented, crushed, and strangled.
>
> The American multimillionaires . . . have profited more than all the rest. . . . They have grabbed hundreds of billions of dollars. And every dollar is sullied [dirtied] with filth: the filth of the secret treaties between Britain and her "allies."

Document 4

In January 1917, British intelligence agencies intercepted this message being sent from the German Foreign Minister to the government of Mexico. It was turned over to the United States Department of State and released to the newspapers in mid-March.

> In the event [that the United States is drawn into the war] we make Mexico a proposal of alliance on the following basis: make war together, make peace together, generous financial support and an understanding on our part that Mexico is to reconquer the lost territory in Texas, New Mexico, and Arizona.

Document 5

These are excerpts from President Wilson's war message to Congress on April 2, 1917.

> On the third of February last I officially laid before you the extraordinary announcement of the Imperial German Government that on and after the first day of February it [would] use its submarines to sink every vessel that sought to approach . . . Great Britain . . . or the western coasts of Europe. . . . The new policy has swept every restriction aside. . . . The present German submarine warfare against commerce is a warfare against mankind.

(continued)

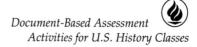

Document-Based Assessment
Activities for U.S. History Classes

DBQ 16: Why Did We Enter World War I? *(continued)*

Document 6

During the four days of Congressional debates following President Wilson's war message, Senator George Norris of Nebraska spoke against voting for war. In this excerpt from his speech of April 4, 1917, he suggested a cause of America's entrance into the war.

> To whom does war bring prosperity? War brings prosperity to the stock gambler on Wall Street—to those who are already in possession of more wealth than can be realized or enjoyed. . . . Their object in having war and in preparing for war is to make money. Human suffering and the sacrifice of human life are necessary, but Wall Street considers only the dollars and the cents. . . . We are going into war upon the command of gold.

Document 7

Here is an excerpt from a secondary source, a major study of the factors that eventually led the United States to abandon neutrality. The excerpt describes President Wilson's thinking during the weeks following Germany's January 31, 1917 resumption of unrestricted submarine warfare. (From Ernest R. May, *The World & American Isolation, 1914–1917*, Harvard University Press, 1959, p. 430, 432–433.)

> . . . chauvinism [pro-war nationalism] was visibly on the rise. The Zimmerman telegram and the sinking of the Cunard liner *Laconia*, with three Americans among the lost, had created a spreading excitement. The *Literary Digest* [a popular magazine] reported newspapers all over the country to be joining in a clamor for war. . . . Future incidents would meanwhile strengthen and embitter the chauvinists. Other *Laconias* were certain to sink. Even as Wilson sat meditating in the White House, five American ships went down.
>
> On March 19 he emerged from his solitude, still anxious and troubled but apparently satisfied that the alternatives of acquiescence [submission] and armed neutrality were impossible. . . . On March 20 he conferred with the cabinet. No one had any alternatives to suggest. The neutralist members . . . were now . . . sure that war was the only course. The Attorney General and the Secretary of Labor seconded the arguments for it. When the President asked the Postmaster General to speak, Bureleson said quietly: "We are at war. I am in favour of asking Congress at the earliest possible moment." . . . The cabinet was one. On the following day the President summoned Congress to meet on April 2.

Document-Based Assessment
Activities for U.S. History Classes

Grading Key

Document 1

Secretary of State Bryan was warning President Wilson against allowing American banks to loan money to any of the countries at war. He was worried that if American financial interests became "allied" with one of these countries, they would use their influence to support that country's war policies in order to ensure repayment of the loans. Bryan, and many others, feared that "economic ties" to England and France might eventually lead the United States into war to protect the loans and other economic interests.

Document 2

This graph supports Bryan's fears. Between 1914 and 1917 American trade and economic links with Britain and France rose tremendously, while trade with Germany fell to virtually nothing. The graph seems to echo Bryan's implied question: Will American investment in the allied nations lead us into war on their side?

Document 3

This 1918 communication by Lenin lends additional credence to the idea that American banks and other financial interests drew the United States into the war to protect their money and enrich American millionaires. (It is good to note how this argument reflects a Marxist viewpoint and justifies Bolshevik Russia's decision to drop out of the war.)

Document 4

The release of the Zimmerman Note in March 1917 enraged Americans; it convinced many that war could no longer be avoided, and that Germany was our enemy.

Document 5

In this excerpt from President Wilson's war message, he pointed to Germany's declaration of submarine warfare as the primary cause of war.

Document 6

Nebraska Senator George Norris was a leading isolationist and opponent of war with Germany. Norris (like the sources of Documents 1–3) saw the influence of big business and finance behind Wilson's call for war.

Document 7

Historian Ernest May believed that Wilson was a sincere pacifist whose patience finally ended with Germany's declaration of submarine warfare and with the inevitability of growing public support for war as American merchant ships were sunk by German U-boats. The unanimity of Wilson's cabinet was a further sign to the president that there was no other choice but war.

Additional Information Beyond the Documents

The documents provide students with only fragments of evidence. Answers should include relevant information from beyond just the documents—information that students have learned from their classroom study. The following list suggests some of the concepts, people, and events that students could include in their essays from their outside learning.

moral diplomacy	Triple Alliance	Triple Entente
British blockade	German U-boats	German-Americans
Robert La Follette	propaganda	freedom of the seas
Sussex pledge	armed neutrality	Ford's peace ship

Unit 9: Prosperity and Depression: Between the Wars

DBQ 17: A National Clash of Cultures in the 1920's

Historical Context:

The census of 1920 revealed some worrisome data. It showed that, for the first time in history, a majority of Americans lived in urban areas. This news was disturbing to many who still lived in rural settings, on farms, or in small towns. They became even more anxious as the decade saw an increase in the farm-to-factory migration that had begun in the early days of the industrial revolution. Rural Americans were concerned. They could understand the lure of the big city, with its bright lights, excitement, and comforts, but this only added to their distrust of cities and of city ways. The growth and prosperity of the cities, contrasted to the decline and despair of America's rural countryside, seemed to announce the passing of an era. Country folk feared that their future was being lost to the culture of the cities. Traditional rural values were being subverted by new, modern city values. America was being assaulted by jazz, materialism, immorality, and fast, brash city ways. Automobiles, radios, movies, advertising, consumer credit, and other new realities of modern life were spreading these dangerous ideas and destroying traditional American values. Traditional, small-town America was under attack by the sinful ways of modernity.

Rural America, feeling under siege, fought back in what became a culture war. The "battles" were fought in the newspapers, schools, churches, movies, music, radio shows, and political campaigns of the decade. And though the forces of urban growth proved largely unstoppable, and the ultimate triumph of modern values was predictable, even today, eighty years later, remnants of this clash of cultures, urban versus rural, modern versus traditional, continue to mark our own lives and times.

◆ **Directions:** The following question is based on the accompanying documents (1–6). As you analyze the documents, take into account both the source of the document and the author's point of view. Be sure to:

1. Carefully read the document-based question. Consider what you already know about this topic. How would you answer the question if you had no documents to examine?

2. Now, read each document carefully, underlining key phrases and words that address the document-based question. You may also wish to use the margin to make brief notes.

3. Based upon your own knowledge of the topic and on the evidence found in the documents, formulate a thesis that directly answers the question.

4. Organize supportive and relevant information into a brief outline.

5. Write a well-organized essay proving your thesis. The essay should be logically presented and should include information both from the documents and from your own knowledge outside of the documents.

> **Question:** *Describe the urban-rural culture wars of the 1920's and the issues over which they were fought.*

(continued)

DBQ 17: A National Clash of Cultures in the 1920's *(continued)*

Document 1

The Ku Klux Klan was first born in the South during the years following the Civil War. At that time, the Klan fought against efforts to give newly-freed slaves full citizen status. Sixty years later, during the 1920's, the Klan rose again, attaining its largest membership ever—approaching five million. The Klan of the 1920's continued the racist anti-African American practices of the earlier Klan. It also expanded its hatred and opposition to Catholics, Jews, immigrants, and others who it believed were enemies of traditional Americanism. The following is an excerpt from an article by a Klan leader. (From H. W. Evans, "The Klan's Fight for Americanism," *North American Review,* March-April-May, 1926.)

> We are a movement of the plain people. . . . We are demanding . . . a return of power into the hands of the everyday . . . average citizen of the old stock. Our members and leaders are all of this class. . . . This is undoubtedly a weakness. It lays us open to the charge of being "hicks" and "rubes" and "drivers of second hand Fords."
>
> Presently we began to find that we were dealing with strange ideas . . . [a] moral breakdown that has been going on for two decades. One by one all our traditional moral standards went by the boards, or were so disregarded that they ceased to be binding. The sacredness of our Sabbath, of our homes, of chastity, and finally even of our right to teach our own children in our own schools fundamental facts and truths were torn away from us.
>
> We found our great cities and the control of much of our industry and commerce taken over by strangers, who stacked the cards of success and prosperity against us.
>
> So the Nordic American today is a stranger in large parts of the land his fathers gave him.

Document 2

One of the most engaging histories of the 1920's is *Only Yesterday: An Informal History of the 1920's* by Frederick Lewis Allen (Harper & Row, 1929, 1964). The following excerpt from this book (p. 168) describes the 1925 case of John Scopes, a young biology teacher in Dayton, Tennessee, who was charged with violating the state law prohibiting the teaching of evolution.

> There was something to be said for the right of the people to decide what should be taught in their tax-supported schools, even if what they decided upon was ridiculous. . . . In the eyes of the public, the trial was a battle between Fundamentalism on the one hand and twentieth century skepticism (assisted by Modernism) on the other. . . .
>
> It was a strange trial. Into the quiet town of Dayton flocked gaunt Tennessee farmers and their families in mule-drawn wagons and ramshackle Fords; quiet, godly people in overalls and gingham and black, ready to defend their faith against the "foreigners," yet curious to know what this new-fangled evolutionary theory might be.

(continued)

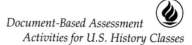

DBQ 17: A National Clash of Cultures in the 1920's *(continued)*

Document 3

Here is an excerpt from a letter written to the national Crime and Law Enforcement Commission in 1929 by an officer of the New England Club of Seattle, Washington. (This letter comes from the National Archives and is found in "The 1920's: A Supplemental Teaching Unit" published by the National Archives and Social Issues Resources Series, Inc. [SIRS])

> . . . much the greater part of the vicious forms of crime are committed by recent immigrants who have not yet learned the necessity for conforming to the statutes and restrictions of our government, and especially those who are subject to certain alien political church influences.
>
> . . . the increase of crime is . . . from . . . the great increase of criminal opportunity afforded by the invention of the auto. . . . And in close connection . . . lie all of the evils of the liquor traffic and drinking. For the liquor evils, sporting business and professional men, fashionable society and a certain type of newspapers are almost wholly responsible.

Document 4

This excerpt comes from an article in a small town newspaper, the Elizabethton, Tennessee *Star*, April 18, 1925. (Found in the SIRS, National Archives 1920's unit.)

> Edward J. Tobin, superintendent of Cook county schools and in that capacity supervisor over the schooling of 100,000 children, believes that "a young couple, a bottle of moonshine and an automobile are the most dangerous quartet that can be concocted for the destruction of human society."

Document 5

This document comes from a letter written by "a mother" to George Wickersham in 1929. Wickersham, a prominent lawyer and former U.S. Attorney General, served as chairman of a committee appointed by President Hoover to investigate prohibition. (This letter, dated July 22, 1929, comes from the National Archives and is found in the SIRS 1920's unit.)

> Please hear the plea of a heartbroken mother and send some reliable person to investigate the condition of an Italian joint, where children are sold rum for ten cents a drink. . . . I am alone trying to rear [my son] an honorable American but how can I when this foreigner . . . is allowed to ruin my boy.

(continued)

*Document-Based Assessment
Activities for U.S. History Classes*

DBQ 17: A National Clash of Cultures in the 1920's *(continued)*

Document 6

This cartoon was published in the *Chicago Daily Tribune*, August 23, 1924.

Grading Key

Document 1

The KKK of the 1920's tried to defend traditional, rural values against the modern, "strange" ideas coming from urban America. This statement suggested that immigrants were to blame for many of these dangerous ideas. A tone of bitterness and class anger ran through this KKK message. The economic hard times of their members' rural lives was blamed on those "strangers" in the cities who "stacked the cards of success and prosperity against us."

Document 2

The Scopes "Monkey Trial" of 1925 was a significant episode in the urban-rural arguments of the 1920's. It pitted the "modernists," who accepted evolutionary theory, against the "traditionalists," who went so far as to legally ban evolution from public schools—requiring instead that biology teachers teach the Christian Biblical creation story. Just as in Document 1, the traditionalists accuse the modernists of being "foreign" or un-American.

Document 3

This letter strongly expresses rural prejudices of the 1920's, blaming immigrants, automobiles, the media, liquor, "fashionable society," and "alien political Church influences" (suggesting the Roman Catholic Church) for the crime wave of the 1920's.

Document 4

To some extent, then, as now, the "culture battle" was generational. The young were more likely to embrace values and practices that traditionalists feared would destroy "human society."

Document 5

This distraught mother feared that her efforts to raise her son to be an "honorable American" were being corrupted by a "foreigner" and by "rum."

Document 6

Just as in Document 4, this cartoonist saw some of the traditionalist-versus-modernist argument as generational. The "toys" of the modern, younger generation represented many of the values which the traditionalists condemned.

Additional Information Beyond the Documents

The documents provide students with only fragments of evidence. Answers should include relevant information from beyond just the documents—information that students have learned from their classroom study. The following list suggests some of the concepts, people, and events that students could include in their essays from their outside learning.

flappers	speakeasies	fads
lost youth	H. L. Mencken	Red scare
normalcy	immigration restriction	William Jennings Bryan
Prohibition	Billy Sunday	Clarence Darrow
Harding	Coolidge	1928 presidential election
Hoover	Al Smith	McNary-Haugen Bill
Lindbergh	Harding scandals	Nineteenth Amendment
Sacco and Vanzetti	Robert La Follette	assembly line production

Unit 9: Prosperity and Depression: Between the Wars

DBQ 18: The New Deal's Opponents

Historical Context:

Today, almost two generations after his death, President Franklin Delano Roosevelt's place in history is secure. FDR is remembered as one of America's greatest presidents, the man who successfully guided the nation through both the Great Depression and World War II. His New Deal program profoundly changed our nation. Social Security, the abolition of child labor, the federal minimum wage, the right of laboring men and women to organize unions and bargain collectively for better wages and working conditions, TVA and rural electrification, federal deposit insurance to protect savings accounts—these are parts of the New Deal, bene-fiting Americans even today. These and other, now expired, New Deal programs helped millions of Americans. It's little wonder that FDR was elected president four times.

And yet, though FDR was loved by millions, he and his policies were also strongly opposed by many others. For some, their hostility toward FDR could accurately be described as hatred. In fact few, if any, presidents inspired such deep anger and scorn. In order to understand FDR, his programs, and his legacy in American history, we need to learn more about those who opposed his New Deal programs and why so many of them grew to hate him so.

◆ **Directions:** The following question is based on the accompanying documents (1–7). As you analyze the documents, take into account both the source of the document and the author's point of view. Be sure to:

1. Carefully read the document-based question. Consider what you already know about this topic. How would you answer the question if you had no documents to examine?

2. Now, read each document carefully, underlining key phrases and words that address the document-based question. You may wish to use the margin to make brief notes.

3. Based upon your own knowledge of the topic and on the evidence found in the documents, formulate a thesis that directly answers the question.

4. Organize supportive and relevant information into a brief outline.

5. Write a well-organized essay proving your thesis. The essay should be logically presented and should include information both from the documents and from your knowledge outside of the documents.

> **Question:** *Identify those groups that most strongly opposed the New Deal and explain the reasons for their opposition.*

(continued)

DBQ 18: The New Deal's Opponents (continued)

Document 1

This political cartoon, "Pinched for Reckless Driving," was published by the Chicago *Tribune* on June 3, 1935.

Document 2

President Roosevelt made this statement in November of 1935.

I can realize that gentlemen in well-warmed and well-stocked clubs will [complain about] the expenses of Government because . . . their Government is spending money for work relief.

(continued)

DBQ 18: The New Deal's Opponents *(continued)*

Document 3

U.S. Senator Huey Long, from Louisiana, became a vocal critic of FDR and of the New Deal during Roosevelt's first term, in the depths of the Depression. Before being elected to the Senate, Long had served as governor of Louisiana. He had built a nationwide following among the poor for his vocal attacks on the rich and powerful. In 1932 Long formulated a "Share-The-Wealth" program, advocating very high tax rates on the rich and on large inheritances to finance social programs to benefit the poor. By 1935, his program and his appeal made Long a political force throughout the nation. He planned to run for president in 1936 against FDR, but in September of 1935 he was assassinated. The following excerpt comes from a radio speech Long made in January of 1935 that was later printed in the *Congressional Record*.

We are in our third year of the Roosevelt depression, with the conditions growing worse . . .

We must now become awakened! We must know the truth and speak the truth. There is no use to wait three more years. It is not Roosevelt or ruin; it is Roosevelt's ruin.

When I saw him [FDR] spending all his time . . . with the business partners of Mr. John D. Rockefeller, Jr., with such men as the Astors, etc., maybe I ought to have had better sense than to have believed he would ever break down their big fortunes to give enough to the masses to end poverty. . . .

So therefore I call upon the men and women of America to immediately join in our work and movement to share our wealth.

1. The fortunes of the multimillionaires and billionaires shall be reduced so that no one person shall own more than a few million dollars. . . .

2. We propose to limit the amount any one man can earn in one year or inherit to $1 million. . . .

3. . . . we will throw into the government Treasury the money and property from which we will care for millions of people who have nothing . . . we will provide a home and the comforts of home, with such common conveniences as radio and automobile, for every family in America, free of debt.

4. We guarantee food and clothing and employment for everyone who should work by shortening the hours of labor to thirty hours per week, maybe less, and to eleven months per year, maybe less. . . .

5. We would provide education . . . for every child . . . through college and vocational education. . . .

6. We would give a pension to all persons above sixty years of age. . . .

7. . . . we would grant a moratorium on all debts which people owe that they cannot pay.

(continued)

*Document-Based Assessment
Activities for U.S. History Classes*

DBQ 18: The New Deal's Opponents *(continued)*

Document 4

In December 1935, *Fortune* magazine ran an article entitled "The Case Against Roosevelt." *Fortune*, a magazine that generally presented a pro-business viewpoint, was read by well-educated professionals and business managers. The following excerpt comes from this article.

> What the business grievance comes down to in the last analysis is that the government of Mr. Roosevelt is a government of men and not of laws. . . . the menace of dictatorship and the essence of dictatorship is government by personal will. What happens when a dictator, either fascist or communist, takes over is that a man or group of men undertake to make a direct attack on social and economic problems. The appeal of the dictator is: "Let us save ourselves! Let us act!" . . . the Roosevelt theory of federal administration is a menacing and dangerous thing.

Document 5

The following cartoon was printed in the June 1936 issue of *Current History*.

WOULDN'T PAUL REVERE BE SURPRISED?

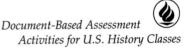

—*Detroit*

(continued)

*Document-Based Assessment
Activities for U.S. History Classes*

DBQ 18: The New Deal's Opponents *(continued)*

Document 6

Former president Herbert Hoover, who had been defeated by FDR in the 1932 presidential election, said the following in a speech given in October of 1936, in the closing days of that year's presidential election.

> Through four years of experience this New Deal attack upon free institutions has emerged as the [most significant] issue in America. [This attack includes] . . . coercion and compulsory organization of men . . . great trade monopolies and price-fixing through codes . . . "economic planning" to regiment and coerce the farmer . . . national plans to put the government into business in competition with its citizens . . . currency inflation . . . attempts to centralize relief in Washington for politics and social experimentation. . . .

Document 7

In 1937, soon after his second inaugural, FDR proposed a law that aimed to change the makeup of the Supreme Court. During his first term, the court had ruled a number of New Deal programs to be unconstitutional. FDR, in an effort to reshape the court to make it more favorable to New Deal legislation, now proposed that he be allowed to appoint a number of new justices, expanding the size of the court. He presented it to the public as a reform, designed to reduce the workload of those justices over the age of 70. But Congress, and much of the public, opposed the "reform," and it never became law. The following is an excerpt from a public statement written in February 1937 by Frank Gannett, owner and publisher of a chain of newspapers. (This letter is filed in the records of the U.S. Justice Dept. See *Teaching With Documents: Using Primary Sources From the National Archives.*)

> President Roosevelt has cleverly camouflaged a most amazing and startling proposal for packing the Supreme Court. . . . Increasing the number of judges from nine to fifteen would not make this high tribunal [court] act any more promptly than it does now, but it would give the President control of the Judiciary Department.
>
> This proposal should give every American grave concern for it is a step toward absolutism and complete dictatorial power.

Grading Key

Document 1

Many people were angered by what they perceived as the New Deal's "disrespect" for, and violation of, the Constitution. This cartoonist showed the police officer (Constitution) arresting the New Dealers (note the negative caricature of the intellectual "professors"). Note also the fast convertible that the New Dealers drove and the old-fashioned bicycle driven by the "cop." While the poor and desperate may have applauded the New Deal's rapid exercise of broad presidential and congressional powers, the conservatives feared and opposed these actions. They were thankful for a conservative Supreme Court which enforced the Constitutional limitation of presidential powers.

Document 2

FDR was convinced that most of his opponents were the rich and comfortable, people who could not appreciate the urgency of the economic crisis or the needs of the millions of unemployed and desperate citizens. (FDR also realized that it was "good politics" to publicly attack the selfishness of the wealthy.)

Document 3

While many of FDR's detractors were wealthy conservatives who condemned the New Deal's radicalism, there were others, like Huey Long and his supporters, who felt that the New Deal was too conservative and had not done enough to aid the poor and the unemployed. In this document, Long attacked FDR for "spending all his time" with Rockefeller and other wealthy friends. He advocated a radical plan to confiscate most of the personal wealth through taxation and then distribute it to the poor. Though this appeared to be a socialist proposal, most historians see Long's radicalism more as a perverted populism and demagoguery.

Document 4

American leaders of commerce and industry generally opposed FDR and the New Deal, and many came to hate and fear what they saw as dictatorial efforts to control free enterprise and socialist efforts to redistribute income. The harsh comparison to fascist or communist dictatorship alluded to Germany's Hitler and the Soviet Union's Stalin, two dictators about whom Americans of the 1930's were anxious and wary.

Document 5

This cartoonist is poking fun at the wealthy, many of whom supported the Liberty League and its attacks on FDR and the New Deal. Their pretension as "patriots" warning America against the dangers of the New Deal's "communist" radicalism is ironically compared to the famous ride of Paul Revere.

Document 6

Hoover summarized many of the complaints of FDR's opponents in this brief excerpt. FDR's New Deal violated free enterprise, regimented the economy, centralized political and economic control in Washington, and involved itself in economic planning and social experiments. (The allusion to European dictatorships was obvious in this attack on the New Deal.)

Document 7

FDR's "court packing" proposal confirmed, for his opponents, what they had claimed for four years—that FDR and the New Deal's efforts at presidential "dictatorship" threatened the constitutional separation of powers and checks and balances. (Perceptive students may note that even many of FDR's friends opposed his "court reform.")

Additional Information Beyond the Documents

The documents provide students with only fragments of evidence. Answers should include relevant information from beyond just the documents—information that students have learned from their classroom study. The following list suggests some of the concepts, people, and events that students could include in their essays from their outside learning.

the Hundred Days	Brain Trust	NRA
Bank Holiday	PWA	WPA
AAA	Direct Relief	Father Coughlin
Dr. Francis Townshend	"Traitor to his class"	Henry Wallace
Harry Hopkins	CCC	Wagner Act
Butler and *Schechter* cases	sit-down strikes	FDIC
SEC	TVA	

Unit 10: America's Last 50 Years

DBQ 19: How Has America Changed Since 1950?

Historical Context:

The last half century has been a time of great and rapid social change for Americans. We emerged from World War II anxious about the growing threat from the Soviet Union. Americans were also anxious about the likelihood of an economic crisis and return to the prewar depression. Millions of soldiers were demobilized and sent home, hoping to soon find work and eager to get on with their lives. The year 1946 saw more marriages occur than any other year in history. And, with the aid of the GI Bill, most GI's found their way into colleges, trade schools, or jobs within a few months of returning home. The feared depression did not occur. In fact, most Americans enjoyed prosperity and economic opportunities like never before. Marriages, growing families, a housing boom in the suburbs, widespread family ownership of autos and TV's, the advent of fast food restaurant chains—these and much more uniquely marked the decade just after the war. The trends and directions of the following 50 years were set. Postwar America launched the tremendous social changes that today, more than 50 years later, describe our lives and define our society.

◆ **Directions:** The following question is based on the accompanying documents (1–8). As you analyze the documents, take into account both the source of the document and the author's point of view. Be sure to:

1. Carefully read the document-based question. Consider what you already know about this topic. How would you answer the question if you had no documents to examine?

2. Now, read each document carefully, underlining key phrases and words that address the document-based question. You may wish to use the margin to make brief notes.

3. Based upon your own knowledge of the topic and on the evidence found in the documents, formulate a thesis that directly answers the question.

4. Organize supportive and relevant information into a brief outline.

5. Write a well-organized essay proving your thesis. The essay should be logically presented and should include information both from the documents and from your knowledge outside of the documents.

Question: *How is American society today different from what our grandparents' generation knew in the years just after World War II?*

(continued)

Document-Based Assessment Activities for U.S. History Classes

DBQ 19: How Has America Changed Since 1950? *(continued)*

Document 1

The following graph shows the divorce rates over the past several decades.

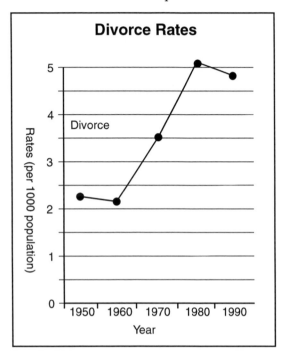

Document 2

Urban, rural, and suburban population of the United States, 1950 and 1995:

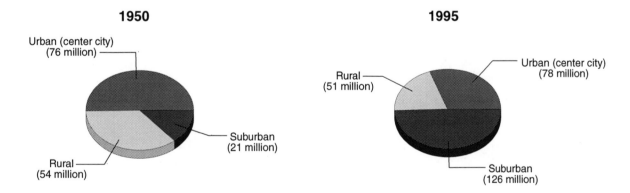

(continued)

DBQ 19: How Has America Changed Since 1950? *(continued)*

Document 3

Here is a memory of middle-class life in a Long Island suburb of New York City in the early 1950's, from Doris Kearns Goodwin's *Wait Till Next Year* (Simon & Schuster, 1997, pp. 66–68).

Our neighborhood life converged on a cluster of stores at the corner of our residential area: the drugstore and butcher shop; the soda shop, which sold papers, magazines, and comics; the delicatessen; and the combination barber shop and beauty parlor. The storekeepers were as much a part of my daily life as the families who lived on my street. When I entered the drugstore for a soda, or went into the delicatessen to buy some potato salad for my mother, the proprietors would greet me by name. . . . Since the families who operated these stores also owned them, their work was more than just a job; it was a way of life. The quality of the goods they sold was as much a [display] of their pride and self-respect as my father's lawn was to him. The personal services they provided were not motivated merely by a desire for good "customer relations" but by their felt relationship to the larger community which they served and looked upon as neighbors. For our mothers, these neighborhood stores supplied all the goods they needed in the course of an ordinary day, and provided a common meeting place where neighbors could talk, trade advice, and gossip as they relaxed over an ice-cream soda or a cup of coffee.

Document 4

The following graphs illustrate how the lives of women and mothers have changed over the past several decades.

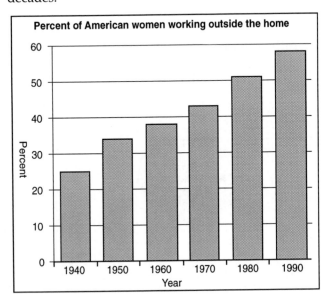

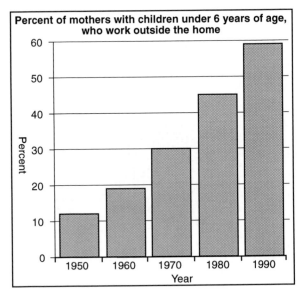

(continued)

Document-Based Assessment
Activities for U.S. History Classes

DBQ 19: How Has America Changed Since 1950? *(continued)*

Document 5

Per capita personal income, 1940–1990	
Current $	Constant $*
1940 $ 570	$ 4,600
1950 $ 1,360	$ 6,400
1960 $ 1,950	$ 7,650
1970 $ 3,200	$10,800
1980 $ 7,800	$13,275
1990 $14,390	$15,900

*Inflation is eliminated and values are shown in 1992 dollars

Document 6

Age distribution within the total population

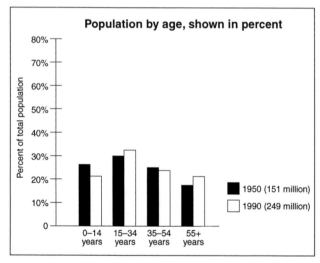

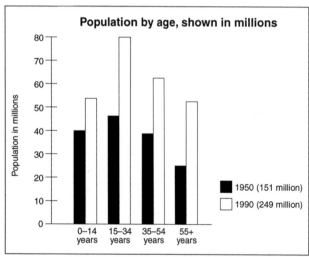

(continued)

*Document-Based Assessment
Activities for U.S. History Classes*

DBQ 19: How Has America Changed Since 1950? *(continued)*

Document 7

Number of youth arrested, 18 years old and younger, 1950 and 1995

1950	208,000
1995	2,085,000

Document 8

The American Economy and Employment, 1950 and 1995

Leading Sectors of the National Economy

1950

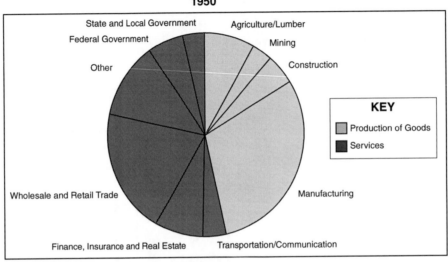

1995

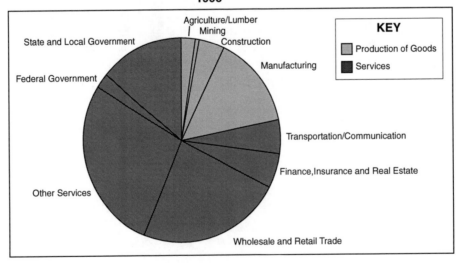

Document-Based Assessment
Activities for U.S. History Classes

Grading Key

Document 1

There is a stark contrast in the divorce rates, which almost doubled over this time.

Document 2

Today most Americans live in suburbia, while in 1950 only one in every seven did. Few Americans today live in small towns or in urban neighborhoods. Some students will compare this document to the description in Document 3.

Document 3

The personal sense of community that Doris Kearns Goodwin remembered from her youth is very different from what most Americans know today. Some students will contrast this description with their lives—huge supermarkets, malls, chain restaurants, impersonal relationships, etc. Especially good answers will note the decline of "downtowns" as neighborhood stores, restaurants, and theaters closed—unable to compete with the national chains, suburban malls, and multiscreen movie theaters. Some may also note the decline in the work ethic and pride in service, contrasted with Goodwin's memory of the early 1950's.

Document 4

Women, and even mothers of young children, are much more likely to be working outside the home today than they were in mid-century. Some students will note that this means that children are much more likely today to be raised by strangers and in institutions.

Document 5

The average American standard of living is much higher today than at mid-century.

Document 6

These charts clearly show the "aging of America" as the postwar babies grow into middle and old age. Today there are more than twice as many older Americans than there were 50 years ago.

Document 7

Students will note this statistic! Some will explain it away (incorrectly) by arguing that there were many more youth in 1995 than in 1950. Good answers will relate this sign of social alienation to the other factors noted—working mothers, decline of personal neighborhoods, etc. Some will see this (correctly) simply as an index of rising national crime.

Document 8

Our economy has changed radically over the past 50 years. Industrial manufacturing has declined greatly. Services clearly dominate today's economy, and increasingly we've moved from an economy that "makes things" to one that "sells and services things," from a society of farms and factories to one of malls. (Some students and teachers may find the governmental statistics of special interest, defying the commonly held belief that the federal government has grown too large in recent history. Actually, as a percentage of the workforce, federal government employment has fallen by half in the past five decades, while state and local government payrolls—and expenditures—have quadrupled.)

Additional Information Beyond the Documents

The documents provide students with only fragments of evidence. Answers should include relevant information from beyond just the documents—information that students have learned from their classroom study. The following list suggests some of the concepts, people, and events that students could use in their essays from their outside learning.

post-war baby boom	suburbanization	television
impact of automobiles	decline of extended families	decline of neighborhoods
homogenization of life	William Levitt	interstate highways
women's rights	birth control	day care centers
McDonald's and fast food	teen employment	mass advertising
Civil Rights movement	computers	environmental movement
foreign trade competition	materialism	affluence

Name_____ Date_____

Unit 10: America's Last 50 Years

DBQ 20: The Civil Rights Movement—America's Second Reconstruction

Historical Context:

The "first" Reconstruction, following the Civil War, failed in its efforts to secure full citizenship rights for the four million African Americans newly freed from slavery. The promises of the Emancipation Proclamation and the Thirteenth, Fourteenth, and Fifteenth Amendments were never truly realized. Within only a few years, racism, economic coercion, violence, and social tradition forced most freedmen into a demeaning second-class citizenship. This was marked by sharecropping, racial segregation, and disfranchisement, enforced by Jim Crow state and local laws. As late as 1900, fully a generation after the Civil War, 90 percent of African Americans remained in the Jim Crow South, where most lived in dire poverty, denied even the most basic civil rights.

Because the "first" Reconstruction failed to bring full and equal citizenship to African Americans, a "second" Reconstruction was necessary. With its roots in the 1930's and 1940's, the Civil Rights movement flowered in the 1950's and 1960's and resulted in real and lasting progress for all Americans. This "second" Reconstruction had a number of origins. The New Deal and especially the efforts of First Lady Eleanor Roosevelt gave hope to African Americans. So too did World War II and its aftermath. (The injustice and inhumanity of Hitler's racist policies and, by implication, of our own racial caste system, touched a raw nerve in those who professed a democratic creed.) The massive northern migration of African Americans, beginning in the 1920's and accelerating in the post-World War II years, made their plight into a national issue after being confined mainly to the South for centuries. Of course, many other people and events played major roles in the Civil Rights movement. For example:

- The political efforts of Presidents Truman, Kennedy, and Johnson
- Brave actions of individuals like Rosa Parks and James Meredith; of groups of young students staging "sit-ins" to force restaurants to serve them; and of freedom riders, forcing bus lines to abide by court orders ending racial segregation policies
- Supreme Court decisions such as the famous *Brown v. Board of Education,* which found racial segregation of public schools to be in violation of the U.S. Constitution
- The impact of television which forced Americans to directly confront the realities of its racist practices on the nightly news
- The leadership of Dr. Martin Luther King, Jr. and other African-American ministers who showed Americans the immorality of racial injustice

Dr. King, and many others involved in the Civil Rights movement, demonstrated the power of eloquence, the impact of the spoken word, the ability to touch the conscience of Americans, to convince people to change, to do what was right. Throughout America's history the mastery and command of writing and speaking have been proven time after time. Thomas Paine's pamphlets, Washington's "Farewell Address," Daniel Webster's "Seventh of March" speech, William Jennings Bryan's "Cross of Gold" speech, the works of the progressive muckrakers, Woodrow Wilson's "Fourteen Points," FDR's "Four Freedoms," Ronald Reagan's expressions of confidence and faith in America's future—these and hundreds of other examples of the power of language fill our history.

Language, written and spoken, provided the authority, power, and force of America's Second Reconstruction: the Civil Rights movement of the 1950's and 1960's. The following documents are some prominent examples of the eloquence and inspiration of the Civil Rights movement.

(continued)

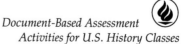

Document-Based Assessment
Activities for U.S. History Classes

DBQ 20: The Civil Rights Movement— America's Second Reconstruction (continued)

◆ **Directions:** The following question is based on the accompanying documents (1–8). As you analyze the documents, take into account both the source of the document and the author's point of view. Be sure to:

1. Carefully read the document-based question. Consider what you already know about this topic. How would you answer the question if you had no documents to examine?

2. Now, read each document carefully, underlining key phrases and words that address the document-based question. You may wish to use the margin to make brief notes.

3. Based upon your own knowledge of the topic and on the evidence found in the documents, formulate a thesis that directly answers the question.

4. Organize supportive and relevant information into a brief outline.

5. Write a well-organized essay proving your thesis. The essay should be logically presented and should include information both from the documents and from your knowledge outside of the documents.

Question: *The rhetoric and prose of the Civil Rights movement aimed to convince white Americans to support the cause of equal rights for African Americans by abolishing segregation and Jim Crow laws. What themes did the champions of civil rights use in their appeal?*

Document 1

Throughout our history, foreign visitors have come to America to study. Many of them have written perceptive and important books about America's people, places, and values. In the 1940's a Swedish sociologist named Gunnar Myrdal came here to study American race relations. His book, *An American Dilemma*, published in 1944, made a significant contribution to the Civil Rights movement. What theme or themes does he address in the following brief excerpt from that book? (From Gunnar Myrdal, *An American Dilemma*, Harper, 1944, pp. 1020–1021.)

> The treatment of the Negro is America's greatest and most conspicuous scandal. It is tremendously publicized . . . for the colored people all over the world . . . this scandal is salt in their wounds.
>
> . . . the bright side is that the conquering of color caste in America is America's own innermost desire. This nation early laid down as the moral basis for its existence the principles of equality and liberty. . . .

(continued)

Document-Based Assessment Activities for U.S. History Classes

DBQ 20: The Civil Rights Movement— America's Second Reconstruction (continued)

Document 2

The 1954 Supreme Court decision, *Brown v. Board of Education* of Topeka, Kansas, was a turning point in American history, an immensely important episode in the story of the Civil Rights movement. Voting nine to zero, the justices ruled segregation of public schools to be in violation of the U.S. Constitution and ordered its end. As you read the following excerpts from the decision, examine the arguments it made against racial discrimination and segregation.

> We come then to the question presented. Does segregation of children in public schools solely on the basis of race, even though the physical facilities and other "tangible" factors may be equal, deprive the children of the minority group of equal educational opportunities? We believe that it does.
>
> . . . We conclude that in the field of public education the doctrine of "separate but equal" has no place. Separate educational facilities are inherently unequal. Therefore, we hold that the plaintiffs and others similarly situated for whom the actions have been brought are, by reason of the segregation complained of, deprived of the equal protection of the laws guaranteed by the Fourteenth Amendment.

Document 3

In the late summer of 1957, a small group of African-American children tried to enter the all-white Central High School in Little Rock, Arkansas. A federal court ordered local and state authorities to protect the rights of these students to integrate the school. Instead, the state governor ordered the Arkansas National Guard to block their entrance. Furthermore, he and other white officials worsened the situation by provoking a dangerously unstable mob of whites who threatened the safety of the African-American children. On September 24, to restore law and order and to force the schools to comply with the court order, President Eisenhower took control of the Arkansas National Guard. He ordered it and U.S. marshals to protect the children and to ensure their right to attend the school. On that evening, President Eisenhower addressed the nation on radio and television. This is an excerpt from that speech.

> At a time when we face grave situations abroad because of the hatred that Communism bears toward a system of government based on human rights, it would be difficult to exaggerate the harm that is being done to the prestige and influence . . . of our nation. We are portrayed [by the Communists] as a violator of those standards of conduct which the peoples of the world united to proclaim in the Charter of the United Nations. There they affirmed "faith in fundamental human rights" and "in the dignity and worth of the human person" and they did so "without distinction as to race, sex, language or religion."
>
> . . . And so, with deep confidence, I call upon the citizens of the state of Arkansas to assist in bringing to an immediate end all interference with the law and its processes. If resistance to the federal court orders ceases at once . . . Thus will be restored the image of America and of all its parts as one nation, indivisible, with liberty and justice for all.

(continued)

DBQ 20: The Civil Rights Movement— America's Second Reconstruction *(continued)*

Document 4

Dr. Martin Luther King, Jr., was a young Baptist minister in an African-American church in Montgomery, Alabama. He came to national prominence in 1955 as the leader of a boycott of the city-owned bus line in protest of its discrimination against African-American riders. From this time on, until he was murdered in 1968, Dr. King remained the most prominent African-American civil rights leader. King advocated nonviolent protest of unjust, racist laws, a doctrine growing from the teachings of Jesus Christ and the Indian independence leader Mohandas Gandhi. King's leadership of demonstrations and open defiance of racist laws led police to arrest him a number of times. While in the Birmingham, Alabama, jail in the spring of 1963, King wrote an eloquent defense of his belief in nonviolent resistance. This excerpt comes from that essay. (From "Letter from Birmingham Jail, April 16, 1963," from *A Testament of Hope: The Essential Writings of Martin Luther King, Jr.,* ed. James M. Washington, Harper & Row, 1986, pp. 289, 291–294.)

My dear Fellow Clergymen,

While confined here in the Birmingham city jail, I came across your recent statement calling our present activities "unwise and untimely." Seldom, if ever, do I pause to answer criticism of my work and ideas. . . . But since I feel that you are men of genuine good will and your criticisms are sincerely set forth, I would like to answer your statement. . . .

. . . You express a great deal of anxiety over our willingness to break laws. This is certainly a legitimate concern. . . . The answer is found in the fact that there are two types of laws: there are JUST and there are UNJUST laws. I would agree with Saint Augustine that "An unjust law is no law at all."

. . . A just law is a man-made code that squares with the moral law of the law of God. An unjust law is a code that is out of harmony with the moral law. . . . Any law that degrades human personality is unjust. All segregation statutes [laws] are unjust because segregation distorts the soul and damages the personality . . .

. . . One who breaks an unjust law must do it OPENLY, LOVINGLY (not hatefully as the white mothers did in New Orleans when they were seen on television screaming, "nigger, nigger, nigger"), and with a willingness to accept the penalty.

(continued)

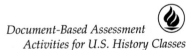

DBQ 20: The Civil Rights Movement— America's Second Reconstruction *(continued)*

Document 5

Freedom marches, freedom rides, sit-ins, and other episodes of the Civil Rights movement were usually accompanied by songs. Many of these songs dated back to slavery days, and many were adaptations of spiritual hymns. Here are excerpts from two of these songs.

WE SHALL OVERCOME

We shall overcome,
   we shall overcome,
We shall overcome some day.
Oh, deep in my heart, I do believe,
We shall overcome some day.

The Lord will see us through,
   the Lord will see us through,
The Lord will see us through today.
Oh, deep in my heart, I do believe.
We shall overcome some day.

[Ludlow Music, Inc., New York, NY]

KEEP YOUR EYES ON THE PRIZE

Paul and Silas, bound in jail,
Had no money for to go their bail.
Chorus:
Keep your eyes on the prize,
Hold on, hold on,
Hold on, hold on—
Keep your eyes on the prize
   Hold on, hold on.

Paul and Silas began to shout,
The jail door opened and they walked out

We're gonna ride for civil rights,
We're gonna ride, both black and white.

We've met jail and violence too,
But God's love has seen us through.

(continued)

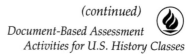

Name_____ Date_____

DBQ 20: The Civil Rights Movement— America's Second Reconstruction (continued)

Document 6

In June of 1963, two African-American students were refused admission to the University of Alabama. A federal court ruled that they should be allowed to enroll in the university. The state governor openly resisted the court order. President Kennedy sent U.S. marshals and troops to see that the law was enforced. This tense confrontation threatened to break out in violence, and to try to calm the situation, President Kennedy spoke to the nation on television. This excerpt comes from that speech.

> I hope that every American, regardless of where he lives, will stop and examine his conscience about this and other related incidents. This nation was founded by men of many nations and backgrounds. It was founded on the principle that all men are created equal and that the rights of every man are diminished when the rights of one man are threatened.
>
> We are confronted primarily with a moral issue. It is as old as the Scriptures and is as clear as the American Constitution.
>
> We preach freedom around the world, and we mean it, and we cherish our freedom here at home; but are we to say to the world, and much more importantly, to each other that this is a land of the free except for the Negroes; that we have no second-class citizens except Negroes; that we have no class or caste system, no ghettoes, no master race except with respect to Negroes?

Document 7

In August 1963, over 200,000 people met in Washington, D.C., to speak out for civil rights, and for political and economic opportunities for African Americans. That year marked the 100th anniversary of Lincoln's issuance of the Emancipation Proclamation. To commemorate this, a huge rally was held in front of the Lincoln Memorial. It was here that Dr. King made his famous "I Have a Dream" speech. Here are some excerpts from that speech.

> I have a dream that one day this nation will rise up and live out the true meaning of its creed: "We hold these truths to be self-evident; that all men are created equal."
>
> Let freedom ring. . . .
>
> When we let freedom ring, when we let it ring from every village and every hamlet, from every state and every city, we will be able to speed up that day when all of God's children, black men and white men, Jews and Gentiles, Protestants and Catholics, will be able to join hands and sing in the words of the old Negro spiritual, "Free at last! Free at last! Thank God Almighty, we are free at last."

(continued)

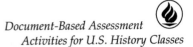

Document-Based Assessment
Activities for U.S. History Classes

DBQ 20: The Civil Rights Movement— America's Second Reconstruction (continued)

Document 8

Though the Fifteenth Amendment, ratified in 1870, had promised African Americans the right to vote, Southern Jim Crow laws made it almost impossible for this right to be exercised. By the year 1900, authoritative estimates guessed that only a few hundred African-American men voted regularly in Southern elections. Even as late as 1964, fewer than one-third of the eligible African-American voters in the South were registered to vote; in some rural counties, almost none dared even to try to register.

In the winter of 1965, President Lyndon Johnson asked Congress to pass a Voting Rights Act that would provide federal assistance and protection to ensure that African Americans would be allowed to register and vote. On the evening of March 15, 1965, he spoke to a joint session of Congress (and to the nation on television) to seek support for this act. These excerpts come from that speech.

I speak tonight for the dignity of man and the destiny of democracy. I urge every member of both parties, Americans of all religions and of all colors, from every section of this country, to join me in that cause.

. . . Our fathers believed that if this noble view of the rights of man was to flourish, it must be rooted in democracy. The most basic right of all was the right to choose your own leaders. The history of this country in large measure is the history of expansion of that right to all of our people.

Many of the issues of civil rights are very complex and most difficult. But about this there can and should be no argument. Every American citizen must have an equal right to vote. There is no reason which can excuse the denial of that right. There is no duty which weighs more heavily on us than the duty we have to ensure that right.

Yet the harsh fact is that in many places in this country men and women are kept from voting simply because they are Negroes.

. . . our duty must be clear to all of us. The Constitution says that no person shall be kept from voting because of his race or his color. We have all sworn an oath before God to support and to defend that Constitution. We must now act in obedience to that oath.

115

Grading Key

Document 1

Myrdal described the "treatment of the Negro" as America's greatest scandal. At a time when the "colored people" of the world were seeking independence and nationhood, America's race issue was hurting her reputation in the world. Myrdal called on Americans to live up to the moral principles of equality and liberty.

Document 2

While Myrdal appealed to moral principles, the Supreme Court decision appealed to Constitutional principles—specifically the Fourteenth Amendment's guarantee of "equal protection of the laws."

Document 3

President Eisenhower appealed to Cold War concerns, saying that the communist nations would condemn the United States for violating the basic beliefs of democracy and the "faith in fundamental human rights" which all United Nations members proclaimed in the UN Charter. He was appealing to American patriotism, asking that we "restore the image of America" in the world.

Document 4

Dr. King, as a clergyman, was appealing to moral principles, and justified his advocacy of nonviolent civil disobedience by describing Jim Crow laws as "unjust" and immoral laws, which contradicted the "moral law" and "the law of God." Teachers may want to emphasize with students the importance of traditional Christian principles to the entire Civil Rights movement. Many of the major leaders of the movement, like Dr. King, were clergymen.

Document 5

These songs also emphasized the significance of African-American religious beliefs to the Civil Rights effort.

Document 6

President Kennedy appealed to patriotism, to democratic American principles, to Christian morality (the Scriptures), and Constitutional rights.

Document 7

Dr. King appealed to American democratic principles, quoting the Declaration of Independence. He also alluded to religious principles, the equality of all of "God's children."

Document 8

President Johnson appealed to Americans' sense of fair play and to the democratic principles upon which our nation was built. The right to vote was, he argued, the most basic of democratic values. He tried to touch the conscience of the members of Congress, reminding them of their oath to God to support the Constitution, which guarantees all Americans the right to vote.

Additional Information Beyond the Documents

Teachers (and students) will find that this DBQ exercise is largely self-contained. Because the DBQ asks students to analyze the prose and rhetoric of the Civil Rights movement, few answers will go much beyond the documents included here. This is especially true if the exercise is used as an in-class assignment.

Nonetheless, it is expected that students will include "contextual" information in their essays. They may, for instance, mention the following:

grandfather clauses	literacy tests	A. Philip Randolph
white citizens councils	1964 election	desegregation of Armed Forces
Plessy v. Ferguson	Executive Order 8802	Civil Rights Act of 1964
George Wallace	Medgar Evers	Malcolm X

Unit 11: Today and Tomorrow—Your Place in History

DBQ 21: What Then Is the American?

Historical Context:

Over two centuries ago, Hector St. John de Crèvecoeur, a French visitor to America, tried to answer this question. Every generation since has renewed and reasked the question. Who are we Americans? What do we and our country really stand for? Is there, as so many Americans have believed, a divine purpose for our country and its people? What, if any, are the values and beliefs that unite us and give definition to our nationality? As we begin the twenty-first century, we ask again: What then is the American?

◆ **Directions:** The following question is based on the accompanying documents (1–8). As you analyze the documents, take into account both the source of the document and the author's point of view. Be sure to:

1. Carefully read the document-based question. Consider what you already know about this topic. How would you answer the question if you had no documents to examine?

2. Now, read each document carefully, underlining key phrases and words that address the document-based question. You may wish to use the margin to make brief notes.

3. Based upon your own knowledge of the topic and on the evidence found in the documents, formulate a thesis that directly answers the question.

4. Organize supportive and relevant information into a brief outline.

5. Write a well-organized essay proving your thesis. The essay should be logically presented and should include information both from the documents and from your knowledge outside of the documents.

> **Question:** *What values and beliefs unite Americans and define our nation and its purpose?*

Document 1

One of the very first expressions of "American values" was made by the Puritan leader John Winthrop in 1630, just before he and his followers landed in Massachusetts. This is an excerpt from his speech.

> Now the only way . . . to provide for our posterity is to follow the counsel of Micah: to do justly, to love mercy, to walk humbly with our God. For this end, we must be knit together in this work as one man . . . in brotherly affection. . . . We must . . . make others' conditions our own, rejoice together, mourn together, labor and suffer together; always having before our eyes our . . . community as members of the same body.

(continued)

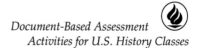

*Document-Based Assessment
Activities for U.S. History Classes*

DBQ 21: What Then Is the American? *(continued)*

Document 2

Hector St. John de Crèvecoeur wrote his *Letters from a Pennsylvania Farmer* during the period of the American Revolution. The following are excerpts from his "letters."

> Here are no aristocratical families . . . no kings . . . no great refinements of luxury. The rich and the poor are not so far removed from each other as they are in Europe.
>
> . . . We are all animated with the spirit of an industry [hard work] which is . . . unrestrained, because each person works for himself.
>
> . . . we are the most perfect society now existing in the world. Here man is free as he ought to be. . . .
>
> . . . The American is a new man, who acts upon new principles. . . . This is an American.

Document 3

The Declaration of Independence, written by Thomas Jefferson, was unanimously approved by the Continental Congress on July 4, 1776. Every year Americans celebrate this document and this occasion as Independence Day.

> We hold these truths to be self-evident, that all men are created equal, that they are endowed by their Creator with certain unalienable rights, that among these are life, liberty and the pursuit of happiness.

Document 4

Ronald Reagan served as president from 1981 to 1989. The following is an excerpt from his State of the Union Address given in January of 1984.

> The heart of America is strong, it's good, and true. . . . We're seeing rededication to bedrock values of faith, family, work, neighborhood, peace, and freedom—values that help bring us together as one people, from the youngest child to the most senior citizen. . . .
>
> . . . America's best days, and democracy's best days, lie ahead. We are a powerful force for good. With faith and courage, we can perform great deeds and take freedom's next step. And we will. We will carry on the traditions of a good and worthy people who have brought light where there was darkness, warmth where there was cold, medicine where there was disease, food where there was hunger, and peace where there was bloodshed.
>
> . . . Let us be sure that those who come after will say [that] . . . we finished the race, we kept them free, we kept the faith.

(continued)

*Document-Based Assessment
Activities for U.S. History Classes*

DBQ 21: What Then Is the American? *(continued)*

Document 5

American income data

Income of households by various characteristics (1992)	
Characteristic	**Median household income**
White African American Hispanic	$32,400 $18,600 $22,800
Female head of household Married couple	$18,600 $42,150
Non-graduate of high school High school graduate College graduate Master's degree Professional degree	$17,400 $29,000 $49,500 $58,000 $85,000

Document 6

Crime in America, various data (1992 statistics)

- Nationwide there were 22,540 murders; 68 percent of victims were shot.
- The murder rate in the United States is three times higher than in Canada and eight times higher than in Japan. The robbery rate in the United States is almost 100 times higher than in Japan.
- Over four million Americans were in jail or prison, on parole, or on probation.
- 90 percent of criminals are males under the age of 45.

(continued)

Document-Based Assessment
Activities for U.S. History Classes

DBQ 21: What Then Is the American? *(continued)*

Document 7

Money spent annually by Americans (1992)	
Books	$ 2.9 billion
Symphony orchestra attendance	.4 billion
Movies	44.0 billion
CD's, records, music videos	12.4 billion
Guns and hunting	3.0 billion
Sporting goods	12.4 billion
Donations to charities	23.5 billion
Restaurants and bars	182.0 billion

Document 8

On the evening of July 15, 1979, President Jimmy Carter spoke to the nation on television about what he called a "crisis of confidence" in modern America. Here are excerpts from that speech.

. . . It is a crisis of confidence. . . . We can see this crisis in the growing doubt about the meaning of our own lives and in the loss of unity of purpose for our Nation.

. . . Our people are losing . . . faith, not only in government itself but in the ability as citizens to serve as the ultimate rulers and shapers of our democracy.

. . . In a nation that was proud of hard work, strong families, close-knit communities and our faith in God, too many of us now tend to worship self-indulgence and consumption. Human identity is no longer defined by what one does, but by what one owns.

. . . there is a growing disrespect for government and for churches and for schools, the news media, and other institutions. This is not a message of happiness or reassurance, but it is the truth and it is a warning.

. . . We are at a turning point in our history. There are two paths to choose. One is the path . . . that leads to fragmentation and self-interest. Down that road lies a mistaken idea of freedom, the right to grasp for ourselves some advantage over others. That path would be one of constant conflict between narrow interests ending in chaos and immobility. It is a certain route to failure.

. . . the traditions of our past, all the lessons of our heritage, all the promises of our future point to another path, the path of common purpose and the restoration of American values. That path leads to true freedom for our Nation and ourselves.

Grading Key

Document 1

Winthrop called on his followers to create a society that would be just, merciful, and humble before God, one where individuals would focus on the needs and concerns of their neighbors and community.

Document 2

Crèvecoeur celebrated America's freedom, a land where no man had to bow before kings or nobles. Because "each person works for himself," America is "animated" with a spirit of hard work.

Document 3

Jefferson believed that the core values of America could be summed up in these "unalienable rights—life, liberty and the pursuit of happiness."

Document 4

Reagan expressed confidence that the essential values of America—"faith, family, work, neighborhood, peace, and freedom"—were strong and vital, that America's and democracy's best days were yet to come.

Document 5

Students will reach various conclusions from these data. Some will bemoan the "inequality" of these incomes, seeing in this a betrayal of America's egalitarian principles. Some will interpret the relationship of education to income as a fulfillment of America's value in opportunity.

Document 6

Again, students will find different "truths" in these data. (Be ready to challenge knee-jerk expressions of prejudices.) Most students will see in these data signs of societal pathology—America's disposition toward violence and lawlessness. Some will use these data to question the validity of "American" principles such as peace, justice, opportunity, and law.

Document 7

It is interesting to see how students use these data. As with the two preceding documents, different students will see different things. But, many will see confirmation of Carter's fears as stated in Document 8— validation of a growing selfishness, materialism, personal indulgence. Some may perceive an apparent American anti-intellectualism.

Document 8

Some students will use this as their primary evidence, sharing Carter's fears that self-indulgence, consumption, self-interest, and a desire to "grasp for ourselves some advantage over others," increasingly define Americans and their dominant values. But as authoritative as a president might be, students need to cite hard data and provide evidence to buttress their opinions.

Additional Information Beyond the Documents

The documents provide students with only fragments of evidence. Answers should include relevant information from beyond just the documents—information that students have learned from their classroom study. This document-based question invites students to state and defend a personal opinion, drawing on their full year of formal study of American history, on contemporary national issues and concerns, and on their own personal life experiences. Perhaps more than any other DBQ in this book, this question is designed to elicit the widest variety of viewpoints from the students in the class. In grading student essays, assess the strength of their thesis, the authority of their evidence, and the persuasiveness of their arguments. Good answers will incorporate most of the documents, but also include much additional data and documentation.

Name_____   Date_____

Unit 11: Today and Tomorrow—Your Place in History

DBQ 22: What Does the Future Hold for You?

Historical Context:

In his Inaugural Address, President Reagan told us that ". . . we are too great a nation to limit ourselves to small dreams," and called on Americans to "renew our faith and our hope" and to "dream heroic dreams." We have been a confident and hopeful people. Polls today (summer of 1998) tell us that 70 percent of Americans see a bright future for themselves and for their children. Typically, this is how it has been in the past, each generation living with better health and greater comforts than their parents. Perhaps this will be true in your future, too. Perhaps your generation will continue to "dream heroic dreams."

Predicting the future, like forecasting the weather, is chancy at best. Looking into the near future can be reasonably accurate, but longer views into a distant future are much less clear. But we can, with some accuracy, draw on our past, identifying those patterns and trends likely to continue and pointing us toward our destiny.

This document-based question asks you to look at your future by examining historic trends, drawing on your own knowledge of America's past and connecting it with your "own dreams."

◆ **Directions:** The following question is based on the accompanying documents (1–7). As you analyze the documents, take into account both the source of the document and the author's point of view. Be sure to:

1. Carefully read the document-based question. Consider what you already know about this topic. How would you answer the question if you had no documents to examine?

2. Now, read each document carefully, underlining key phrases and words that address the document-based question. You may wish to use the margin to make brief notes.

3. Based upon your own knowledge of the topic and on the evidence found in the documents, formulate a thesis that directly answers the question.

4. Organize supportive and relevant information into a brief outline.

5. Write a well-organized essay proving your thesis. The essay should be logically presented and should include information both from the documents and from your knowledge outside of the documents.

Question: *Look ahead 25 years into your future. Predict the economic and social challenges and realities that you and other Americans will be facing at that time.*

(continued)

         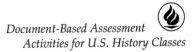
Document-Based Assessment
Activities for U.S. History Classes

DBQ 22: What Does the Future Hold for You? *(continued)*

Document 1

Selected Marriage/Family Data and Trends

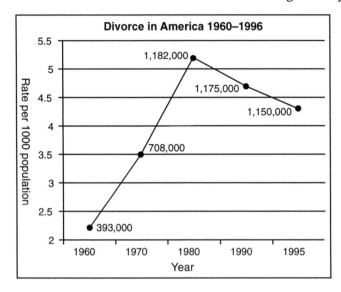

Divorce in America 1960–1996

Rate per 1000 population

1,182,000
1,175,000
1,150,000
708,000
393,000

Births to unmarried women (as a percentage of all American births)	
1950	4%
1960	5%
1970	11%
1980	18%
1990	28%
1995	32%

Document 2

Ethnic / racial population trends, 1950 –1995				
Year	Percent White	Percent Hispanic*	Percent African-American	Percent Asian, Native-American, Others
1950	89%	NA	10%	NA
1960	88.5%	NA	10.5%	1%
1970	87.5%	NA	11%	1%
1980	86%	6.4%	12%	2.3%
1990	84%	9%	12%	4%
1995	83%	10%	13%	5%

* Note that persons of Hispanic origin may be of any race.

(continued)

Document-Based Assessment
Activities for U.S. History Classes

DBQ 22: What Does the Future Hold for You? *(continued)*

Document 3

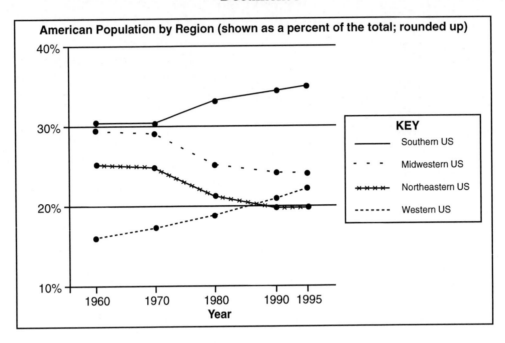

American Population by Region (shown as a percent of the total; rounded up)

KEY
— Southern US
---- Midwestern US
×××× Northeastern US
...... Western US

Document 4

U.S. Population by Selected Age Groups, 1960–1997				
Year	Ages 0–19 (in millions)	Percent of Total	Ages 45 and older (in millions)	Percent of Total
1960	69.2	38.4	52.2	29.3
1970	77.1	37.9	61.8	30.4
1980	72.5	32	68.2	30.1
1990	71.8	28.9	77.3	31.1
1997	76.9	28.8	89.3	33.4

(continued)

DBQ 22: What Does the Future Hold for You? (continued)

Document 5

SELECTED INCOME STATISTICS

Average annual income by educational attainment, 1975–1996					
	1975	**1985**	**1996**	**1996***	**Real Increase (Decrease)**
Non-graduate of high school	$ 7,000	$10,500	$14,000	$19,250	(–$5,250)
High school graduate	$ 8,500	$15,000	$21,400	$23,400	(–$2,000)
Some college/Associate degree	$ 9,000	$17,000	$25,000	$24,750	+$ 250
Bachelor's degree	$12,000	$25,500	$37,000	$33,000	+$4,000
Advanced degree	$17,500	$33,000	$57,000	$48,125	+$8,875

* income needed to match 1975 income (accounting for inflation)

Household income by family characteristics (1995)			
	White	**African American**	**Hispanic**
Married couple families	$47,600	$41,300	$30,200
Single mother households	$24,400	$15,600	$14,800
All families	$43,300	$26,800	$25,500

Document 6

Employment by selected economic sectors, 1960–1995 (shown as a percent of total employment)				
	1960	**1970**	**1980**	**1995**
Mining	1.3%	0.9%	1.1%	0.5%
Construction	5.4%	5.1%	4.8%	4.2%
Manufacturing	31%	27%	22%	15%
Transportation and public utilities	7.4%	6.4%	5.7%	5%
Sales/trade	21%	21%	23%	23%
Various services	14%	16%	20%	29%
Government	15%	18%	18%	17%

Document 7

Medical costs, 1960–1990			
	Total $	**Percent of GNP**	**$ per Household**
1960	$ 27 billion	5.3%	$ 510
1970	$ 74 billion	7.4%	$1,170
1980	$250 billion	9.2%	$3,090
1990	$675 billion	12.2%	$7,250

Grading Key

Document 1

Students, just as do other historians, will "see" different things in these data. Pessimists may decry the demise of the American family and project continued demise into the future. Optimists may point to the apparent decline in the divorce rate in recent years and project better times ahead for family stability.

Document 2

It seems pretty certain that 25 years from now America will be an increasingly diverse and multi-ethnic society.

Document 3

It's likely that America's historic migration to the West and to the Southern "sunbelt" will continue. Some students will predict an acceleration of this trend with the huge increase in the number of older, retired Americans.

Document 4

American society will clearly be "older" 25 years from now as the postwar "baby boomers" become senior citizens. Some students will note that this may presage a crisis of Social Security and private retirement plans and may result in oppressive medical costs for future Americans. Some may foresee a future generational conflict over taxes, rationed medical care, and the like.

Document 5

These data should tell students that their future affluence depends largely on their level of education. Advanced education will be a prerequisite for personal wealth, and those with only a high school diploma or less will likely be unable to live a middle-class lifestyle. Students will use the second set of data in several ways. Some will decry the race-based income inequities; others will note how income levels for families with both parents present are much greater than for single-mother families (another endorsement of family stability).

Document 6

Students should see in these data that relatively few of them will find secure employment in manufacturing (some students may explain how American industrial jobs are being lost to countries with lower labor costs). Services (including professions), sales, and government may employ over three of every four workers 25 years from now.

Document 7

Clearly, medical costs will soon be a crushing burden for Americans if they continue to climb at the rate seen in this chart.

Additional Information Beyond the Documents

Many students will devote most of their essays to predicting how Americans 25 years from now will wrestle with the challenges of escalating medical costs, an aging population, racial/ethnic changes, and the possible social cleavages that could result from growing income inequity.

This DBQ exercise invites students to "connect their own dreams" to the data. Consequently, teachers can expect to read much more "opinion" than in most DBQ essays. Still, students must use pertinent data from these documents plus relevant information from beyond the documents—information that they have learned from their classroom study. The following list suggests some of the concepts and events that students could use in their essays from their outside learning.

causes of "family trends"	factors encouraging ethnic diversity	Sunbelt migration
post-war baby boom	Social Security and retirement crisis	Medicare and Medicaid
NAFTA and free trade	technological revolution	immigration policies
feminism	crime statistics	growing college costs